THE 50 MOST BEAUTIFUL AQUARIUM FISH IN THE WORLD

LOCHLAINN SEABROOK WRITES ACROSS THE FOLLOWING GENRES & TOPICS

Academic	Earth Sciences	Illustrations	Poetry
Acoustic Culture	Ecology	Inspirational	Police Studies
Adventure	Ecotourism	Intellectual History	Politics
Aesthetics	Educational	Interdisciplinary Lost Knowledge	Practical Law
Alternate History	Encyclopediography	Interviews	Prehistoric Art
American Civil War	Entertainment	Journalism	Prehistoric Life
American History	Environmental History	Law Enforcement	Prehistory
American Politics	Environmental Science	Law of Attraction	Preservation Studies
American South	Environmental Studies	Legal Studies	Presidential History
American West	Environmental Tourism	Lexicography	Primatology
Anatomy and Physiology	Epistemology	Life After Death	Primary Documents
Ancient History	Ethnobotany	Life-Stage Biology	Prophecy
Animal Development	Ethnology	Lifestyle	Psychology
Antiquities	Ethology	Literary History	Public Safety
Anthologies	Ethnomusicology	Literature	Quiz
Anthropology	Ethnic Studies	Lost Intellectual Heritage	Quotations
Apocrypha	Etymology	Lost Knowledge Studies	Recollections
Aquariology	European History	Lost Treasures	Reference
Archaeology	Evolutionary Anthropology	Marine Biology	Religion
Art	Evolutionary Biology	Matriarchy	Revolutionary Period
Art History	Evolutionary History	Medical History	Science
Astronomy	Evolutionary Psychology	Memoir	Scripture
Aviation	Exploration	Men's Studies	Self-help
Aviation History	Exobiology	Metahistory	Social Sciences
Behavioral Science	Exposés	Metaphysics	Sociology
Biblical Exegesis	Family Histories	Military	Sound Studies
Biblical Hermeneutics	Field Guides	Military History	Southern Culture
Bioarchaeology	Film	Museum Studies	Southern Heritage
Biography	Folklore	Music History	Southern Narratives
Book History	Forestry	Musicology	Southern Studies
Botany	Genealogy	Mysteries and Enigmas	Southern Traditions
Camping	General Audience	Mysticism	Speeches
Children's Books	Geography	Mythology	Spirituality
Children's Natural History	Geology	National Parks	Spiritualism
Christian Mysticism	Genetics	Natural Health	Sport Science
Citizen's Rights Education	Ghost Stories	Natural History	Symbolism
Civil Liberties	Gospels	Natural Philosophy	Technology
Civil Rights Law	Guidebooks	Natural Science	Thanatology
Civil Self Defense	Handbooks	Nature	Theology
Clinical Studies	Health and Fitness	Nature Appreciation	Theosophy
Coffee Table Books	Heritage Conservation	Nature Art	Tourism
Coloring Books	Heritage Travel	Nonfiction	Travel
Comparative Aesthetics	Hiking	Oceanography	UFOlogy
Comparative Animal Development	Historical Ecology	Onomastics	United States
Comparative History	Historical Fiction	Ontogeny	Vanished Works Studies
Comparative Mythology	Historical Musicology	Outdoor Recreation	Vexillology
Comparative Religion	Historical Nonfiction	Paleoanthropology	Victorian Era Studies
Conservation	Historiography	Paleoecology	Victorian Medicine
Constitutional Law	History	Paleography	Visual Arts
Constitutional Studies	History of Ideas	Paleoichthyology	Visual Cultural Memory Studies
Cooking	History of Medicine	Paleontology	Visual Encyclopediography
Criminal Justice	History of Science	Paleozoology	Visual Natural History
Criminal Procedure	History of Technology	Paranormal	War
Cryptozoology	Hobbies and Crafts	Parapsychology	Western Art Music History
Cultural Anthropology	Human-Animal Relationships	Parks & Campgrounds	Western Civilization
Cultural Geography	Human-Animal Studies	Patriarchy	Wildlife
Cultural Heritage	Human Evolution	Patriotism	Wildlife Biology
Cultural Heritage Studies	Humanities	Performing Arts	Wildlife Photography
Cultural History	Humor	Philosophical Aesthetics	Women's Studies
Cultural Studies	Ichthyology	Philosophy	World History
Cultural Tourism	Illustrated Lost History	Philosophy of Science	Writing
Deep Time Natural History	Illustrated Music History	Photography	Young Adult
Destination Guides	Illustrated Natural History	Physical Anthropology	Zoology
Diet and Nutrition	Illustrated Zoological Anthologies	Pictorial	

Mr. Seabrook does not author books for fame and glory, but for the love of writing and sharing his knowledge.

Be curious, not judgmental.

SeaRavenPress.com

The 50 Most Beautiful

AQUARIUM FISH

In The World

An Illustrated Guide to Nature's Most
Stunning Freshwater and Marine Species

LOCHLAINN SEABROOK

Bestselling Author, Award-winning Historian, Acclaimed Artist

Diligently Researched and Generously Illustrated
by the Author for the Elucidation of the Reader

2025

Sea Raven Press, Park County, Wyoming USA

THE 50 MOST BEAUTIFUL AQUARIUM FISH IN THE WORLD

Published by
Sea Raven Press, LLC, founded 1995
Park County, Wyoming, USA
SeaRavenPress.com

All text, artwork, and illustrations copyright © Lochlainn Seabrook 2025
in accordance with U.S. and international copyright laws and regulations, as stated and protected under the Berne Union for the Protection of Literary and Artistic Property (Berne Convention), and the Universal Copyright Convention (the UCC). All rights reserved under the Pan-American and International Copyright Conventions.

PRINTING HISTORY
1st SRP paperback edition, 1st printing, November 2025 • ISBN: 978-1-955351-74-4
1st SRP hardcover edition, 1st printing, November 2025 • ISBN: 978-1-955351-75-1

ISBN: 978-1-955351-74-4 (paperback)
Library of Congress Control Number: 2026930459

This work is the copyrighted intellectual property of Lochlainn Seabrook and has been registered with the Copyright Office at the Library of Congress in Washington, D.C., USA. No part of this work (including text, covers, drawings, photos, illustrations, maps, images, diagrams, etc.), in whole or in part, may be used, reproduced, stored in a retrieval system, or transmitted, in any form or by any means now known or hereafter invented, without written permission from the publisher. The sale, duplication, hire, lending, copying, digitalization, or reproduction of this material, in any manner or form whatsoever, is also prohibited, and is a violation of federal, civil, and digital copyright law, which provides severe civil and criminal penalties for any violations.

The 50 Most Beautiful Aquarium Fish in the World: An Illustrated Guide to Nature's Most Stunning Freshwater and Marine Species, by Lochlainn Seabrook. Includes an introduction, educational section, notes to the reader, and illustrations.

ARTWORK
Front and back cover design and art, book design, layout, font selection, and interior art by Lochlainn Seabrook.
All images, pictures, photos, illustrations, image captions, graphic design, and graphic art copyright © Lochlainn Seabrook.
All images created and/or selected, placed, manipulated, cleaned, colored, and tinted by Lochlainn Seabrook.
Cover image: "Clownfish Aquarium," copyright © Lochlainn Seabrook.
All rights reserved.

All persons who approve of the authority and principles of Colonel Lochlainn Seabrook's literary work, and realize its benefits as a means of reeducating the world about facts left out of mainstream books, are hereby requested to avidly recommend his titles to others and to vigorously cooperate in extending their reach, scope, and influence around the globe.

The views documented in this book concerning aquariology, tropical fish, and ichthyology are those of the publisher.
PROUDLY WRITTEN, DESIGNED, AND PUBLISHED IN THE UNITED STATES OF AMERICA.

DEDICATION

To one of my favorite freshwater fish, the zebra danio.

Danio rerio. All illustrations copyright © Lochlainn Seabrook.

EPIGRAPH

"The tropical fish hobby combines several different things. It has something of the interest there is in collecting stamps or coins or old prints: you may get rare, or unusually beautiful, or valuable specimens to take pride in, or show your friends.

"It has a little of the pleasure that comes from keeping pets; your fish are alive and interesting, with habits and personalities of their own. There is in it a good deal of the interest that a farmer or pigeon-fancier or kennel-owner gets from raising stock.

"And best of all, particularly for Boy Scouts and those who are interested in natural science, there is a chance to bring a whole miniature outdoor world of little-known plants and living creatures right into your own livingroom for observation and new knowledge."

Myron M. Stearns
Boys' Life, February 1933

One of my saltwater aquariums. Copyright © Lochlainn Seabrook.

CONTENTS

Notes to the Reader ❧ page 11
The Benefits of Keeping Fish, by Lochlainn Seabrook ❧ page 12
Introduction, by Lochlainn Seabrook ❧ page 13

1. Arabian Butterflyfish (*Chaetodon melapterus*) ❧ page 16
2. Banggai Cardinalfish (*Pterapogon kauderni*) ❧ page 18
3. Black Neon Tetra (*Hyphessobrycon herbertaxelrodi*) ❧ page 20
4. Blood Parrot Cichlid (Hybrid *Cichlasoma sp.*) ❧ page 22
5. Blue Discus (*Symphysodon aequifasciatus*) ❧ page 24
6. Blue-Green Chromis (*Chromis viridis*) ❧ page 26
7. Boeseman's Rainbowfish (*Melanotaenia boesemani*) ❧ page 28
8. Cardinal Tetra (*Paracheirodon axelrodi*) ❧ page 30
9. Copperband Butterflyfish (*Chelmon rostratus*) ❧ page 32
10. Coral Beauty Angelfish (*Centropyge bispinosa*) ❧ page 34
11. Dwarf Gourami (*Trichogaster lalius*) ❧ page 36
12. Electric Blue Acara (*Andinoacara pulcher*) ❧ page 38
13. Emperor Angelfish (*Pomacanthus imperator*) ❧ page 40
14. Flame Angelfish (*Centropyge loriculus*) ❧ page 42
15. Flame Hawkfish (*Neocirrhites armatus*) ❧ page 44
16. Freshwater Angelfish (*Pterophyllum scalare*) ❧ page 46
17. Frontosa Cichlid (*Cyphotilapia frontosa*) ❧ page 48
18. Gardner's Killifish (*Fundulopanchax gardneri*) ❧ page 50
19. German Blue Ram (*Mikrogeophagus ramirezi*) ❧ page 52
20. Glass Catfish (*Kryptopterus vitreolus*) ❧ page 54
21. Green Mandarin Dragonet (*Synchiropus splendidus*) ❧ page 56
22. Harlequin Rasbora (*Trigonostigma heteromorpha*) ❧ page 58
23. Jack Dempsey (*Rocio octofasciata*) ❧ page 60
24. Kissing Gourami (*Helostoma temminckii*) ❧ page 62
25. Lined Seahorse (*Hippocampus erectus*) ❧ page 64
26. Lionfish (*Pterois volitans*) ❧ page 66
27. Moorish Idol (*Zanclus cornutus*) ❧ page 68
28. Ocellaris Clownfish (*Amphiprion ocellaris*) ❧ page 70
29. Oscar (*Astronotus ocellatus*) ❧ page 72
30. Pajama Cardinalfish (*Sphaeramia nematoptera*) ❧ page 74
31. Pearl Gourami (*Trichopodus leerii*) ❧ page 76
32. Picasso Triggerfish (*Rhinecanthus aculeatus*) ❧ page 78
33. Powder Blue Tang (*Acanthurus leucosternon*) ❧ page 80
34. Purple Tang (*Zebrasoma xanthurum*) ❧ page 82

35. Queen Angelfish (*Holacanthus ciliaris*) ☙ page 84
36. Raccoon Butterflyfish (*Chaetodon lunula*) ☙ page 86
37. Red Line Torpedo Barb (*Sahyadria denisonii*) ☙ page 88
38. Royal Gramma (*Gramma loreto*) ☙ page 90
39. Sailfin Tang (*Zebrasoma veliferum*) ☙ page 92
40. Scarlet Badis (*Dario dario*) ☙ page 94
41. Siamese Algae Eater (*Crossocheilus oblongus*) ☙ page 96
42. Siamese Fighting Fish (*Betta splendens*) ☙ page 98
43. Six-Line Wrasse (*Pseudocheilinus hexataenia*) ☙ page 100
44. Spotted Mandarin (*Synchiropus picturatus*) ☙ page 102
45. Sunburst Anthias (*Serranocirrhitus latus*) ☙ page 104
46. Tiger Barb (*Puntigrus tetrazona*) ☙ page 106
47. Twinspot Goby (*Signigobius biocellatus*) ☙ page 108
48. Yellow Tang (*Zebrasoma flavescens*) ☙ page 110
49. Zebra Danio (*Danio rerio*) ☙ page 112
50. Zebra Pleco (*Hypancistrus zebra*) ☙ page 114

Meet the Author-Historian-Artist ☙ page 117
Praise for the Author ☙ page 119
Learn More ☙ page 123

Copperband butterflyfish, *Chelmon rostratus*. Copyright © Lochlainn Seabrook.

NOTES TO THE READER

MY SOURCES
☛ As with all of my natural history books, every effort has been made to provide the most current and reliable data available, presented objectively and free of speculation or bias.

MY RESEARCH
☛ Because of the inherent challenges in oceanography, ichthyology, marine biology, and limnology, complete scientific consensus is not always possible. For this reason, my findings may occasionally differ from those of other nature writers or researchers in these fields. In certain instances, specific data have been estimated where definitive values remain uncertain.

DISCLAIMER
☛ In light of the above, and considering the many variables of aquarium environments and individual expertise levels, I cannot guarantee absolute accuracy regarding aspects such as diet, water pH, temperature, salinity, species compatibility, specific gravity, etc. Additionally, since fish coloration and morphology vary widely due to numerous environmental and genetic factors, my illustrations may not always reflect standard hues or forms. This book is intended as a general reference guide only. Readers are encouraged to conduct their own research and tailor care to their particular circumstances.

Green mandarin dragonet, *Synchiropus splendidus*. Copyright © Lochlainn Seabrook.

THE BENEFITS OF KEEPING FISH

Keeping fish is more than a pastime—it's a window into the living artistry of nature. A well-maintained aquarium is a dynamic ecosystem, a tranquil refuge, and a miniature world that teaches balance, patience, and care. For many, it becomes both science and sanctuary—a refuge where beauty flourishes through understanding and application.

BENEFITS OF THE AQUARIUM HOBBY

- Encourages Environmental Awareness: Caring for aquatic life fosters respect for natural ecosystems, reminding us how water quality, light, and temperature sustain life everywhere.
- Teaches Science and Discipline: Monitoring pH, salinity, and filtration introduces chemistry, biology, and environmental balance in an engaging, hands-on way.
- Promotes Calm and Focus: Watching fish swim reduces stress, lowers blood pressure, and restores concentration. Aquariums are used in hospitals, schools, and offices for their calming effects.
- Brings Living Art Into the Home: Few things rival the color and movement of fish. Aquariums turn light, water, and life into a constantly shifting natural masterpiece.
- Offers Educational Value: Children and adults alike learn responsibility, observation, and empathy by maintaining the delicate balance that keeps a tank healthy.
- Connects Us to Nature: Even in urban environments, an aquarium restores our link to the wild and brings the rhythm of the natural world into daily life.
- Encourages Mindfulness: Routine care and quiet observation promote reflection and patience, countering the fast pace of modern life.
- Builds Stewardship: Every aquarist becomes a caretaker of life, learning firsthand that harmony depends on knowledge, discipline, and compassion.

One of my freshwater aquariums. Copyright © Lochlainn Seabrook.

INTRODUCTION

SINCE EARLY CHILDHOOD I HAVE been fascinated by the silent world beneath the water's surface. Over the decades—as both a nature writer and an aquarist—I have devoted countless hours to observing, studying, and caring for fish of every shape and hue. I once even ran my own aquarium-design business, supplying and maintaining custom freshwater and marine systems for homes and offices. Those years taught me not only the science of aquariology, but also the art of creating living ecosystems—balanced, self-sustaining worlds where light, movement, and color merge in natural harmony.

Red line torpedo barb. Copyright © Lochlainn Seabrook.

My book, *The 50 Most Beautiful Aquarium Fish in the World*, is the culmination of a lifetime of that experience. It brings together some of the most visually striking species ever kept in captivity—both freshwater and saltwater—from around the globe. My goal has been to present them as they truly are: living works of art shaped by millions of years of evolution, each adapted to its own ecological niche yet universally captivating to the human eye.

Every profile in these pages combines accurate scientific data with visual realism. Each fish is portrayed in a cinematic, photo-realistic setting that mirrors its natural environment or aquarium equivalent. Measurements, coloration, and behavior are drawn from reliable, peer-reviewed sources as well as my own field and aquarium observations. Rather than exaggerate their appearance for effect, I have sought to honor their genuine beauty—the iridescence of a discus, the elegant glide of a tang, the electric shimmer of a tetra shoal, the graceful poise of an angelfish, the jeweled brilliance of a betta in full display.

It is my hope that these portraits will deepen appreciation for both the science and the artistry of the aquarium hobby. Beyond their aesthetic value, these fish demonstrate nature's infinite creativity and fragility. To maintain them properly we must understand the worlds from which they come. This book is offered in that spirit: as a guide for enthusiasts, a reference for scholars, and a tribute to one of Earth's most enchanting realms—the underwater paradise we bring into our homes.

Lochlainn Seabrook
Park County, Wyoming USA
November 2025

"Books invite all; they constrain none."
Hartley Burr Alexander (1873-1939)

The 50 Most Beautiful
AQUARIUM FISH
in the World

ARABIAN BUTTERFLYFISH

AQUARIUM FISH PROFILE 1
COMMON NAME: Arabian butterflyfish.
SCIENTIFIC NAME: *Chaetodon melapterus*.
HABITAT TYPE: Marine; coral reefs and tropical lagoons.
ORIGIN: Western Indian Ocean; Red Sea to the Arabian Gulf and Gulf of Oman.
SIZE: Up to 5.5 in TL.
LIFESPAN: Up to 10 years in captivity.
COLORATION: Body bright yellow with narrow horizontal orange stripes; face with a black eye-band; caudal fin black edged in iridescent blue. Dorsal, anal, and pelvic fins vivid yellow. Juveniles display a darker head mask and deeper hue.
DIET: Feeds mainly on coral polyps, small benthic invertebrates, and algae; in aquaria accepts mysis shrimp, brine shrimp, and specialized marine pellets. Requires frequent feeding due to metabolism.
TEMPERAMENT: Peaceful toward most species but territorial toward similar butterflyfish.
TANK LEVEL: Mid to upper.
MINIMUM TANK SIZE: 75 gal for one specimen or bonded pair.
AQUARIUM CONDITIONS: Temperature 74–82 °F; pH 8.1–8.4; specific gravity 1.020–1.025; strong filtration and moderate to high water movement required. Prefers aquaria with live rock and ample swimming space.
BEHAVIOR: Active diurnal swimmer; spends much of the day grazing among live rock and corals. Often forms monogamous pairs in the wild. Sensitive to poor water quality and sudden parameter changes.
BREEDING: Oviparous; releases pelagic eggs in pairs at dusk. Captive breeding rare due to larval rearing difficulty and coral-feeding dependence.
COMPATIBLE SPECIES: Reef-safe with caution—monitor behavior around delicate corals; best housed with peaceful tankmates such as gobies, tangs, or wrasses. Avoid aggressive or coral-nipping species such as triggerfish or large angelfish.
DIFFICULTY LEVEL: Advanced.
POPULARITY: Uncommon in the aquarium trade.
NOTABLE FEATURES: Endemic to the Arabian region; one of few butterflyfish with a completely black tail. Valued for its striking color contrast and graceful swimming behavior. Thrives best in mature reef systems with stable conditions.

Arabian butterflyfish, *Chaetodon melapterus*. Copyright © Lochlainn Seabrook.

BANGGAI CARDINALFISH

AQUARIUM FISH PROFILE 2
COMMON NAME: Banggai cardinalfish.
SCIENTIFIC NAME: *Pterapogon kauderni*.
HABITAT TYPE: Marine; calm seagrass beds and coral shallows.
ORIGIN: Endemic to the Banggai Archipelago off Sulawesi, Indonesia, where it inhabits shallow coral reefs, seagrass beds, and sheltered lagoons rich in sea urchins.
SIZE: Commonly 2.5 to 3 in TL.
LIFESPAN: Typically 4 to 5 years in captivity under optimal care.
COLORATION: Silver body with three broad black vertical bars and numerous white spots on fins; elongated rays on the dorsal and caudal fins give a graceful, ornate silhouette when swimming.
DIET: Carnivorous; consumes zooplankton, small crustaceans, and finely chopped marine meaty foods such as mysis shrimp, brine shrimp, and copepods in aquaria.
TEMPERAMENT: Peaceful and shy toward other species but males may become aggressive toward rivals when confined or during breeding.
TANK LEVEL: Mid to upper regions, often hovering motionless near branching coral or long-spined sea urchins for protection.
MINIMUM TANK SIZE: 30 gal for a small group, larger if keeping multiple males.
AQUARIUM CONDITIONS: Temperature 78–82°F; pH 8.1–8.4; salinity 1.020–1.025; moderate flow with stable parameters and excellent filtration.
BEHAVIOR: Slow, deliberate swimmer that prefers quiet surroundings; remains close to structure and avoids strong currents. Active mainly at dusk and night, showing calm schooling behavior in secure environments.
BREEDING: Paternal mouthbrooder; the male incubates up to 30 eggs for about 20 days before releasing fully formed fry that can feed on live foods immediately.
COMPATIBLE SPECIES: Peaceful reef fish such as gobies, blennies, firefish, small wrasses, and seahorses.
DIFFICULTY LEVEL: Moderate; requires consistent feeding, stable salinity, and low stress.
POPULARITY: Highly popular for its striking beauty, calm nature, and success in captive breeding programs worldwide.
NOTABLE FEATURES: Limited natural range and unique reproductive method have made it a model species for marine conservation and sustainable aquaculture efforts.

Banggai cardinalfish, *Pterapogon kauderni*. Copyright © Lochlainn Seabrook.

BLACK NEON TETRA

AQUARIUM FISH PROFILE 3
COMMON NAME: Black neon tetra.
SCIENTIFIC NAME: *Hyphessobrycon herbertaxelrodi*.
HABITAT TYPE: Freshwater; slow, shaded creeks and streams.
ORIGIN: Upper Paraguay River basin, Brazil.
SIZE: Up to 1.6 in TL.
LIFESPAN: About 5 years.
COLORATION: A slender, translucent body marked by a brilliant white stripe above a deep black lateral band; fins often display subtle orange or red hues, especially in mature specimens. The contrast of dark and light gives the fish a glowing, iridescent appearance under subdued aquarium lighting.
DIET: Omnivorous; consumes microcrustaceans, insect larvae, algae, and fine flake or pellet foods. Supplement diet with frozen or live daphnia and brine shrimp for optimal color and health.
TEMPERAMENT: Peaceful and social schooling species that thrives in groups of six or more; its calm nature makes it a reliable choice for community aquariums.
TANK LEVEL: Middle to upper.
MINIMUM TANK SIZE: 15 gal.
AQUARIUM CONDITIONS: Temperature 72–82 °F; pH 5.5–7.5; soft to moderately hard water; dim lighting preferred; dark substrate and live plants enhance colors and reduce stress.
BEHAVIOR: Constant, coordinated swimmer; remains active in open water but retreats to vegetation when startled. Prefers calm companions and minimal current; steady lighting and consistent parameters encourage natural activity.
BREEDING: Egg scatterer; spawning occurs at dawn among fine plants or mesh; eggs hatch in 24 hours; fry feed on infusoria and later micro-worms or brine shrimp. Adults must be removed post-spawn to prevent egg predation.
COMPATIBLE SPECIES: Ideal with peaceful fish such as harlequin rasboras and neon tetras. Avoid fin-nippers like tiger barbs and larger aggressive species.
DIFFICULTY LEVEL: Easy.
POPULARITY: Long-established and widely kept aquarium favorite admired for its durability and subtle elegance.
NOTABLE FEATURES: Distinctive reflective lateral stripe visible even in low light; hardy, adaptable, and especially suited for planted or biotope-style community aquariums, where its quiet beauty enhances group displays.

Black neon tetra, *Hyphessobrycon herbertaxelrodi*. Copyright © Lochlainn Seabrook.

BLOOD PARROT CICHLID

AQUARIUM FISH PROFILE 4
COMMON NAME: Blood parrot cichlid.
SCIENTIFIC NAME: Hybrid *Cichlasoma sp.* (Blood parrot strain).
HABITAT TYPE: Freshwater; warm, slow-moving tropical rivers.
ORIGIN: Artificial hybrid created in Taiwan in the 1980s from Central American *Cichlasoma*-type species.
SIZE: Up to 8 in TL.
LIFESPAN: 10–15 years.
COLORATION: Bright orange to deep red, though yellow and pink forms exist. Body is rounded and laterally compressed with a small, beak-like mouth and large expressive eyes. Fins may be transparent or lightly tinted. Color deepens with maturity and proper diet, especially in males.
DIET: Omnivorous; accepts high-quality pellets, bloodworms, krill, and vegetable matter such as spirulina flakes.
TEMPERAMENT: Semi-aggressive but generally peaceful compared to most large cichlids. Can coexist with similarly sized non-aggressive fish.
TANK LEVEL: Middle to bottom.
MINIMUM TANK SIZE: 55 gal for a single fish or 75 gal for a small group.
AQUARIUM CONDITIONS: Temperature 76–82 °F; pH 6.5–7.5; maintain good filtration, moderate water movement, and frequent water changes. Provide caves, driftwood, and open swimming areas.
BEHAVIOR: Active, intelligent, and social with familiar humans. May rearrange gravel and decorations. Performs mild territorial displays but rarely causes injury.
BREEDING: Difficult; many individuals are sterile. Fertile pairs lay adhesive eggs on flat stones and exhibit typical cichlid guarding behavior. Fry survival is limited.
COMPATIBLE SPECIES: Silver dollars, giant danios, or large tetras. Avoid fin-nippers such as tiger barbs, serpae tetras, rosy barbs, red-tailed sharks, and black skirt tetras.
DIFFICULTY LEVEL: Moderate. Requires stable water and regular maintenance.
NOTABLE FEATURES: Rounded body and small fixed mouth give it a unique look among aquarium cichlids. Known for expressive behavior and bright coloration developed through selective hybridization. Strong, personable disposition makes it a favorite among aquarists seeking an intelligent, interactive companion fish.

Blood parrot cichlid, hybrid *Cichlasoma sp*. Copyright © Lochlainn Seabrook.

BLUE DISCUS

AQUARIUM FISH PROFILE 5
COMMON NAME: Blue discus.
SCIENTIFIC NAME: *Symphysodon aequifasciatus*.
HABITAT TYPE: Freshwater; calm Amazon lakes and creeks.
ORIGIN: Amazon River Basin, South America.
SIZE: Up to 8 in TL.
LIFESPAN: 10–15 years.
COLORATION: The body is round and laterally compressed with iridescent blue and turquoise hues. Fine horizontal stripes run across the flanks, often accented by red or orange highlights in the fins. The eyes are bright red in adults.
DIET: Omnivorous. Eats insect larvae, small crustaceans, worms, and plant material. In aquariums, accepts high-quality flakes, pellets, and frozen foods such as bloodworms and brine shrimp.
TEMPERAMENT: Peaceful but hierarchical within groups. Should be kept in small schools of five or more. Avoid aggressive species such as tiger barbs or redtail sharks.
TANK LEVEL: Middle.
MINIMUM TANK SIZE: 75 gallons for a small group.
AQUARIUM CONDITIONS: Temperature 82–88°F, pH 6.0–6.5, soft water under 4° dGH. Strong filtration with gentle flow and weekly water changes. Prefers subdued lighting and vertical cover such as driftwood or tall plants.
BEHAVIOR: Slow-moving and deliberate. Forms social hierarchies and bonds. Sensitive to stress and rapid water changes. Swims gracefully in open midwater.
BREEDING: Pairs form naturally. Eggs are laid on vertical surfaces and guarded by both parents. Fry feed on skin secretions before transitioning to fine foods. Best success occurs in soft, acidic water near 86°F.
COMPATIBLE SPECIES: Peaceful tankmates such as cardinal tetras, rummy-nose tetras, corydoras catfish, and small plecos.
DIFFICULTY LEVEL: Advanced. Requires pristine water quality and stable conditions.
POPULARITY: Iconic. Among the most admired and sought-after tropical fish worldwide.
NOTABLE FEATURES: Distinguished by its perfectly circular body, vivid blue patterning, and strong parental care, making it a showpiece species in advanced freshwater aquariums. Highly intelligent, recognizes its keeper, and displays individual personality.

Blue discus, *Symphysodon aequifasciatus*. Copyright © Lochlainn Seabrook.

BLUE-GREEN CHROMIS

AQUARIUM FISH PROFILE 6
COMMON NAME: Blue-green chromis.
SCIENTIFIC NAME: *Chromis viridis.*
HABITAT TYPE: Marine; shallow coral lagoons and reef slopes.
ORIGIN: Indo-Pacific region, from the Red Sea and East Africa to French Polynesia and southern Japan.
SIZE: Up to 4 in TL.
LIFESPAN: Typically 6 to 8 years in captivity.
COLORATION: Iridescent blue-green body with subtle silver underglow, becoming more turquoise under aquarium lighting. Fins are translucent with faint blue margins.
DIET: Omnivorous. Consumes plankton, algae, small crustaceans, and prepared aquarium foods such as flakes, pellets, and frozen mysis shrimp.
TEMPERAMENT: Peaceful schooling fish. Best kept in small groups of 6 or more to prevent stress and establish natural hierarchy.
TANK LEVEL: Mid to upper levels.
MINIMUM TANK SIZE: 30 gallons for a small group.
AQUARIUM CONDITIONS: Temperature 75–82°F, pH 8.1–8.4, salinity 1.020–1.025, strong filtration, moderate water flow, and ample open swimming space.
BEHAVIOR: Active, social, and hardy. Displays schooling movements and retreats among live rock when startled. Swims continuously in open water during daylight.
BREEDING: Egg-layer. Males prepare and guard nests on substrate; eggs hatch in 2–3 days. Breeding is uncommon in home aquaria due to larval feeding challenges.
COMPATIBLE SPECIES: Peaceful reef fish such as clownfish, royal gramma, and firefish. Avoid aggressive damselfish and dottybacks.
DIFFICULTY LEVEL: Easy to moderate. Suitable for intermediate marine aquarists.
POPULARITY: Highly popular for reef aquariums due to color, activity, and hardiness.
NOTABLE FEATURES: Exhibits shimmering color changes with light angle. Forms synchronized schools in the wild and displays calm coexistence with most reef inhabitants. Its radiant hues intensify under actinic lighting, making it a focal point in reef displays. The blue-green chromis is also valued for its resilience and adaptability to captive environments, thriving in both reef and fish-only systems.

Blue-green chromis, *Chromis viridis*. Copyright © Lochlainn Seabrook.

BOESEMAN'S RAINBOWFISH

AQUARIUM FISH PROFILE 7
COMMON NAME: Boeseman's rainbowfish.
SCIENTIFIC NAME: *Melanotaenia boesemani*.
HABITAT TYPE: Freshwater; clear, fast-flowing streams and lakes.
ORIGIN: Lakes Ayamaru and Hain in West Papua, Indonesia.
SIZE: Up to 4.5 in TL.
LIFESPAN: 5–8 years.
COLORATION: Distinct two-tone body; front half blue-gray to violet, rear half bright orange to red, divided sharply at mid-body. Fins often edged in iridescent blue or white. Males are more vividly colored, especially during courtship.
DIET: Omnivorous; accepts high-quality flakes, small pellets, brine shrimp, daphnia, and blanched greens.
TEMPERAMENT: Peaceful schooling fish suited for community aquariums. Best kept in groups of six or more to reduce stress and maintain natural color.
TANK LEVEL: Middle to upper levels.
MINIMUM TANK SIZE: 30 gal for small groups; 55 gal or more preferred for adult schools.
AQUARIUM CONDITIONS: Temperature 78–82 °F; pH 7.0–8.0; hardness 10–20 dGH. Provide open swimming space with dense vegetation at edges. Clean, well-oxygenated water is essential.
BEHAVIOR: Active, coordinated, and highly social. Displays dominance and courtship through fin spreading and color intensification. Enjoys current from filters or air stones that simulate natural lake flow.
BREEDING: Egg scatterer among fine plants or spawning mops. Spawns at dawn; parents may consume eggs. Incubation 7–10 days at 80 °F. Fry require infusoria or liquid fry food before transitioning to baby brine shrimp.
COMPATIBLE SPECIES: Harlequin rasboras, pearl gouramis, corydoras catfish, and most tetras. Avoid fin-nippers such as tiger barbs or red-tailed sharks.
DIFFICULTY LEVEL: Moderate.
POPULARITY: Highly popular among rainbowfish species for color contrast, energetic behavior, and adaptability to community tanks.
NOTABLE FEATURES: Exhibits rapid color change with mood and light angle; known for its shimmering, metallic sheen in natural sunlight.

Boeseman's rainbowfish, *Melanotaenia boesemani*. Copyright © Lochlainn Seabrook.

CARDINAL TETRA

AQUARIUM FISH PROFILE 8
COMMON NAME: Cardinal tetra.
SCIENTIFIC NAME: *Paracheirodon axelrodi*.
HABITAT TYPE: Freshwater; soft, acidic blackwater streams and floodplain pools.
ORIGIN: Upper Orinoco and Negro River basins in South America.
SIZE: Up to 2 in TL.
LIFESPAN: 3 to 5 years in captivity.
COLORATION: A vivid blue lateral stripe extends from snout to tail, beneath which runs a brilliant red band from midbody to caudal fin; underparts silver-white. Colors intensify in soft, dimly lit aquariums, especially in groups.
DIET: Omnivorous; consumes fine flake foods, crushed pellets, baby brine shrimp, daphnia, and micro worms.
TEMPERAMENT: Peaceful schooling fish; non-aggressive and shy when kept alone.
TANK LEVEL: Midwater.
MINIMUM TANK SIZE: 15 gallons for a small school of six or more.
AQUARIUM CONDITIONS: Prefers soft, slightly acidic water (pH 5.0–6.5) with temperatures between 74–82°F. Provide subdued lighting, live plants, leaf litter, and dark substrate to replicate natural blackwater. Maintain high oxygenation and stable water chemistry.
BEHAVIOR: Active schooling species; best kept in groups of at least eight to reduce stress. Avoid strong currents. Moves gracefully through plants and driftwood.
BREEDING: Egg scatterer; requires dim light, very soft water (<2 dGH), and temperature near 80°F. Adults should be removed after spawning to prevent egg predation.
COMPATIBLE SPECIES: Ideal with peaceful community fish such as neon tetra, harlequin rasbora, and corydoras catfish; avoid larger or fin-nipping species like tiger barbs or serpae tetras.
DIFFICULTY LEVEL: Moderate due to sensitivity to water chemistry and temperature fluctuations.
POPULARITY: Extremely popular worldwide for its brilliant coloration and calm nature.
NOTABLE FEATURES: Distinguished by continuous red coloration along nearly the entire body length, unlike the neon tetra, which shows partial red.

Cardinal tetra, *Paracheirodon axelrodi*. Copyright © Lochlainn Seabrook.

COPPERBAND BUTTERFLYFISH

AQUARIUM FISH PROFILE 9
COMMON NAME: Copperband butterflyfish.
SCIENTIFIC NAME: *Chelmon rostratus*.
HABITAT TYPE: Marine; coral reefs and rocky coastal areas.
ORIGIN: Indo-Pacific region, from the Andaman Sea to the Great Barrier Reef.
SIZE: Reaches up to 8 in TL.
LIFESPAN: Typically 5–10 years in captivity with proper care.
COLORATION: Silvery-white body with four vertical orange bands and a false eyespot on the rear dorsal fin; long narrow snout.
DIET: Carnivorous; feeds on small crustaceans, worms, coral polyps, and in captivity accepts mysis shrimp, clams, and specialized frozen foods.
TEMPERAMENT: Peaceful but may act territorial toward other butterflyfish.
TANK LEVEL: Middle to lower regions.
MINIMUM TANK SIZE: 75 gallons.
AQUARIUM CONDITIONS: Temperature 75–82 °F; pH 8.1–8.4; salinity 1.020–1.025; well-oxygenated and stable marine setup with live rock for foraging.
BEHAVIOR: Solitary or paired; deliberate swimmer; spends much time probing rock crevices for food; sensitive to poor water quality and sudden changes.
BREEDING: Rarely achieved in captivity; pelagic spawners with eggs and larvae developing in open water.
COMPATIBLE SPECIES: Generally suitable with peaceful marine fish such as gobies, tangs, and wrasses; avoid aggressive species like triggers or large angelfish.
DIFFICULTY LEVEL: Advanced; requires excellent water conditions, varied diet, and stable environment; sensitive to transport stress and competition for food.
POPULARITY: Common in the aquarium trade but often recommended only for experienced aquarists due to feeding challenges.
NOTABLE FEATURES: Long snout adapted for extracting prey from crevices; distinctive orange-banded pattern and false eyespot used for predator confusion; prized for elegance and distinctive behavior. Its presence adds visual balance to reef aquariums and helps control small pest organisms. Represents one of the most recognizable and graceful species among all butterflyfish, admired for both beauty and ecological function in reef systems.

Copperband butterflyfish, *Chelmon rostratus*. Copyright © Lochlainn Seabrook.

CORAL BEAUTY ANGELFISH

AQUARIUM FISH PROFILE 10
COMMON NAME: Coral beauty angelfish.
SCIENTIFIC NAME: *Centropyge bispinosa*.
HABITAT TYPE: Marine; shallow coral reefs and warm lagoons.
ORIGIN: Indo-Pacific region, from East Africa to Central Pacific.
SIZE: Up to 4 in TL.
LIFESPAN: 10–15 years in captivity.
COLORATION: Deep blue body with vivid orange to reddish flanks, thin vertical striping, and iridescent blue edging on the dorsal and anal fins. Color intensity varies slightly by region.
DIET: Omnivore. Consumes algae, marine plants, sponges, and small invertebrates. In captivity, thrives on marine algae, spirulina, mysis shrimp, and high-quality angelfish preparations.
TEMPERAMENT: Semi-aggressive. Generally peaceful toward dissimilar species but territorial toward other dwarf angelfish.
TANK LEVEL: Mid-level to lower regions.
MINIMUM TANK SIZE: 55 gallons.
AQUARIUM CONDITIONS: Temperature 72–82 °F, pH 8.1–8.4, specific gravity 1.020–1.025, moderate to strong water movement, live rock for grazing and hiding.
BEHAVIOR: Active swimmer and constant grazer. May occasionally nip at corals, particularly soft species. Requires ample rockwork and caves to establish territory.
BREEDING: Difficult in captivity. Protogynous hermaphrodite; males develop from dominant females. Spawning occurs in pairs at dusk with external fertilization.
COMPATIBLE SPECIES: Works well with clownfish, gobies, tangs, and wrasses. Avoid housing with aggressive triggers or fin-nippers like sergeant majors and damsels.
DIFFICULTY LEVEL: Moderate.
POPULARITY: Highly popular due to hardiness, coloration, and adaptability.
NOTABLE FEATURES: One of the most durable and vividly colored dwarf angelfish. Recognized for its resilience, compact size, and ability to thrive in both reef and fish-only aquariums. Found singly or in harems in the wild, often grazing continuously on filamentous algae. Adaptable to varied marine environments when water quality is stable, making it a standout choice for vibrant reef displays and long-term marine collections. Its natural balance of color, grace, and endurance makes it a cornerstone species for aquarists seeking beauty with reliability.

Coral beauty angelfish, *Centropyge bispinosa*. Copyright © Lochlainn Seabrook.

DWARF GOURAMI

AQUARIUM FISH PROFILE 11
COMMON NAME: Dwarf gourami.
SCIENTIFIC NAME: *Trichogaster lalius*.
HABITAT TYPE: Freshwater; slow, weedy streams and ponds.
ORIGIN: Slow-moving streams, ponds, and rice paddies of India, Bangladesh, and Pakistan.
SIZE: Up to 3.5 in TL.
LIFESPAN: 4 to 5 years.
COLORATION: Males display vivid turquoise-blue bodies crossed by vertical orange-red bands, with iridescent fins edged in blue. Females are silver-gray with faint striping and less fin coloration. Color intensity increases during courtship and under good lighting.
DIET: Omnivorous; eats small insects, larvae, algae, and fine-grade flakes or pellets. Accepts live or frozen brine shrimp, bloodworms, and daphnia.
TEMPERAMENT: Generally peaceful but males can be territorial toward each other. Best kept singly or as a pair in community aquariums. Avoid aggressive or fin-nipping species such as tiger barbs or serpae tetras.
TANK LEVEL: Middle to upper levels.
MINIMUM TANK SIZE: 15 gal for a pair.
AQUARIUM CONDITIONS: Temperature 77–82 °F; pH 6.0–7.5; soft to moderately hard water; gentle filtration; floating plants and low current preferred.
BEHAVIOR: Calm, deliberate swimmer. Uses its labyrinth organ to breathe air at the surface. Males construct bubble nests beneath floating vegetation and guard eggs.
BREEDING: Easy in warm, still water. Male builds a bubble nest and courts the female beneath it. After spawning, remove the female to prevent aggression. Eggs hatch within 24–36 hours; fry become free-swimming after 3 days.
COMPATIBLE SPECIES: Neon tetras, harlequin rasboras, corydoras catfish, peaceful gouramis, or small livebearers.
DIFFICULTY LEVEL: Moderate.
POPULARITY: Very common in the aquarium trade and prized for its bright color and gentle nature.
NOTABLE FEATURES: Possesses a labyrinth organ enabling it to breathe atmospheric air; one of the smallest and most colorful gouramis. Adaptable to a wide range of well-maintained freshwater aquariums. Known for its graceful movements, shimmering hues, and amity, making it a centerpiece in low-flow community tanks.

Dwarf gourami, *Trichogaster lalius*. Copyright © Lochlainn Seabrook.

ELECTRIC BLUE ACARA

AQUARIUM FISH PROFILE 12
COMMON NAME: Electric blue acara.
SCIENTIFIC NAME: *Andinoacara pulcher*.
HABITAT TYPE: Freshwater tropical rivers and streams with sandy or muddy bottoms.
ORIGIN: Northern South America, from Venezuela and Trinidad to Colombia.
SIZE: Up to 8 in TL.
LIFESPAN: 8–10 years.
COLORATION: Metallic blue with green and turquoise highlights across the body and fins. The head and gill area often display golden or bronze tones, while the fins show faint red margins.
DIET: Omnivorous. Accepts flakes, pellets, frozen, and live foods such as brine shrimp, bloodworms, and insect larvae.
TEMPERAMENT: Generally peaceful but territorial when breeding. Suitable for community tanks with similarly sized calm fish.
TANK LEVEL: Middle to bottom.
MINIMUM TANK SIZE: 40 gallons for a pair.
AQUARIUM CONDITIONS: Temperature 72–82 °F, pH 6.5–8.0, hardness 5–20 dGH. Provide fine substrate, hiding rocks, driftwood, and hardy plants. Maintain stable, clean water with good filtration. Weekly partial water changes are essential for health and color retention.
BEHAVIOR: Active and inquisitive. Recognizes its keeper and interacts with surroundings. Avoid keeping with aggressive species such as oscars or red devils. Can coexist peacefully in a mixed South American setup when given space and cover.
BREEDING: Biparental substrate spawner. The pair cleans a flat surface for egg deposition. Both sexes guard eggs and fry intensely. Fry feed on infusoria and finely crushed food.
COMPATIBLE SPECIES: Angelfish, keyhole cichlids, silver dollars, corydoras catfish, and larger tetras.
DIFFICULTY LEVEL: Easy to moderate.
POPULARITY: High among aquarists for its color, personality, and hardiness.
NOTABLE FEATURES: Displays shimmering iridescence under aquarium lighting and adapts well to community setups. One of the most peaceful cichlids available, prized for its intelligence and strong parental behavior. Calm, resilient, and visually striking, it bridges beauty and manageability in home aquariums.

Electric blue acara, *Andinoacara pulcher*. Copyright © Lochlainn Seabrook.

EMPEROR ANGELFISH

AQUARIUM FISH PROFILE 13
COMMON NAME: Emperor angelfish.
SCIENTIFIC NAME: *Pomacanthus imperator*.
HABITAT TYPE: Marine; coral reefs and tropical reef slopes.
ORIGIN: Indo-Pacific region, from the Red Sea and East Africa to the Hawaiian and Line Islands.
SIZE: Reaches 15 in TL.
LIFESPAN: Averages 15 years in captivity, up to 20 in the wild.
COLORATION: Adults display vivid blue and yellow stripes with a dark eye band and yellow tail; juveniles are deep blue with white and light-blue rings.
DIET: Omnivorous. Consumes sponges, tunicates, and algae in nature; accepts chopped shrimp, marine algae, and prepared angelfish foods in aquaria.
TEMPERAMENT: Semi-aggressive. May dominate tankmates of similar shape or color.
TANK LEVEL: Middle to lower.
MINIMUM TANK SIZE: 180 gallons.
AQUARIUM CONDITIONS: Maintain 72–82°F, pH 8.1–8.4, salinity 1.020–1.025. Provide ample live rock for grazing and shelter.
BEHAVIOR: Territorial and active. May chase smaller or slower fish. Avoid fin-nippers like sergeant majors and aggressive triggerfish. Best kept singly or as a mated pair in very large systems.
BREEDING: Rare in captivity. In nature, forms harems; spawning occurs at dusk with free-floating eggs. Larvae drift pelagically before settling. Juveniles develop adult markings at about 4 in TL.
COMPATIBLE SPECIES: Peaceful tangs, butterflyfish, and smaller wrasses.
DIFFICULTY LEVEL: Advanced. Requires stable conditions and large swimming space. Sensitive to poor water quality and rapid parameter shifts. Regular water changes and balanced diet are essential to maintain full color intensity and prevent fin erosion. Thrives in mature reef tanks with ample grazing surfaces and low nitrate levels.
POPULARITY: Highly sought after for its dramatic color change and regal appearance.
NOTABLE FEATURES: Distinct metamorphosis pattern, bold horizontal bands, and strong body shape distinguish it from all other angelfish. Known as a symbol of tropical reef elegance and one of the ocean's most enduring icons of beauty and grace.

Emperor angelfish, *Pomacanthus imperator*. Copyright © Lochlainn Seabrook.

FLAME ANGELFISH

AQUARIUM FISH PROFILE 14
COMMON NAME: Flame angelfish.
SCIENTIFIC NAME: *Centropyge loriculus*.
HABITAT TYPE: Marine; shallow coral reefs and rubble zones.
ORIGIN: Central and western Pacific Ocean, including the Marshall, Christmas, and Cook Islands.
SIZE: Up to 4 in TL.
LIFESPAN: 7–10 years.
COLORATION: Brilliant orange-red body with vertical black bars and electric blue edging on dorsal and anal fins. Males often show more intense coloration than females.
DIET: Omnivorous; consumes algae, detritus, and small crustaceans. In aquariums, thrives on a mix of marine algae, mysis shrimp, and quality angelfish preparations.
TEMPERAMENT: Semi-aggressive; territorial toward similar dwarf angelfish but generally peaceful with dissimilar species.
TANK LEVEL: Mid to lower levels.
MINIMUM TANK SIZE: 55 gallons.
AQUARIUM CONDITIONS: Temperature 74–82 °F; pH 8.1–8.4; specific gravity 1.020–1.025; moderate current and ample live rock for grazing and shelter.
BEHAVIOR: Active swimmer that spends much time grazing on surfaces. May nip at soft corals or clam mantles if underfed. Displays quick darting movements when startled. Average cruising speed 1–2 mph. Requires shaded retreats to reduce stress.
BREEDING: Pelagic spawner. Pairs form in captivity but successful breeding is rare; eggs are released near dusk and hatch within one day. Larvae are planktonic before settling.
COMPATIBLE SPECIES: Works well with peaceful reef fish such as clownfish, gobies, and wrasses. Avoid housing with aggressive species like damselfish and large triggerfish.
DIFFICULTY LEVEL: Moderate; requires stable water quality and careful diet management.
POPULARITY: Very high; among the most desired dwarf angelfish due to its vivid coloration and manageable size.
NOTABLE FEATURES: Distinctive fiery coloration and vertical barring make this species a standout in reef aquariums. Exhibits complex social and territorial behaviors. Frequently observed cleaning rock surfaces and coral heads in the wild. Native populations remain stable across its range, making it a sustainable and enduring favorite among marine aquarists.

Flame angelfish, *Centropyge loriculus*. Copyright © Lochlainn Seabrook.

FLAME HAWKFISH

AQUARIUM FISH PROFILE 15
COMMON NAME: Flame hawkfish.
SCIENTIFIC NAME: *Neocirrhites armatus*.
HABITAT TYPE: Marine; warm coral reefs with rocky outcrops.
ORIGIN: Central and western Pacific Ocean, including the Hawaiian and Marshall Islands.
SIZE: Up to 4 in TL.
LIFESPAN: Approximately 5–7 years in captivity.
COLORATION: Brilliant red body with darker maroon shading along the dorsal region; eyes ringed in black; fins translucent with red highlights.
DIET: Carnivorous; consumes small crustaceans, shrimp, and other meaty marine foods.
TEMPERAMENT: Semi-aggressive; bold and territorial toward smaller or similarly shaped fish.
TANK LEVEL: Prefers upper and mid-level perches among live rock and coral branches.
MINIMUM TANK SIZE: 30 gallons.
AQUARIUM CONDITIONS: Temperature 75–80°F; pH 8.1–8.4; salinity 1.020–1.025; moderate water movement; excellent filtration and oxygenation.
BEHAVIOR: Perching fish that hops between coral heads rather than swimming continuously; highly alert and observant; known to dart quickly to capture prey.
BREEDING: Rare in captivity; egg-laying species; male and female engage in courtship displays above reef structures; eggs drift with currents.
COMPATIBLE SPECIES: Works well with peaceful tankmates such as clownfish, tangs, and gobies; avoid keeping with cleaner shrimp or small ornamental crustaceans, which it may eat.
DIFFICULTY LEVEL: Moderate; requires stable marine conditions and meaty diet variety.
POPULARITY: Highly prized for its striking color and lively personality; a favorite among reef aquarists worldwide.
NOTABLE FEATURES: Perch-adapted pectoral fins allow it to cling to coral branches; lacks swim bladder, giving it a distinctive hopping movement; renowned for its vivid red hue, large expressive eyes, and constant inquisitive nature. Its bold yet endearing demeanor makes it a standout display fish. Often regarded as one of the most charismatic species in the aquarium trade.

Flame hawkfish, *Neocirrhites armatus*. Copyright © Lochlainn Seabrook.

FRESHWATER ANGELFISH

AQUARIUM FISH PROFILE 16

COMMON NAME: Freshwater angelfish.
SCIENTIFIC NAME: *Pterophyllum scalare*.
HABITAT TYPE: Freshwater; calm Amazon rivers and floodplains.
ORIGIN: Amazon Basin, including the rivers, tributaries, and floodplain lakes of Brazil, Peru, and Colombia.
SIZE: Up to 6 in TL; total height including fins up to 10 in.
LIFESPAN: 8–10 years.
COLORATION: Wild specimens display a silvery body crossed by dark vertical bands with subtle green and blue iridescence. Captive breeding has produced many color morphs such as marble, koi, silver, zebra, and veil-tail, showing combinations of white, gold, orange, black, and metallic tones.
DIET: Omnivorous; consumes insect larvae, small crustaceans, worms, and plant matter. In captivity, thrives on high-quality flakes, pellets, and frozen foods such as brine shrimp and bloodworms.
TEMPERAMENT: Semi-aggressive; calm in youth but territorial and hierarchical when mature, particularly during courtship or spawning.
TANK LEVEL: Mid to upper.
MINIMUM TANK SIZE: 30 gal for a pair; larger aquaria preferred for groups or community setups.
AQUARIUM CONDITIONS: Temperature 76–82°F; pH 6.0–7.5; soft to moderately hard water. Gentle flow, tall vegetation, and vertical décor promote natural behavior.
BEHAVIOR: Moves deliberately with slow, elegant fin strokes. Often forms pair bonds or small groups. Requires clean, stable water and dislikes abrupt disturbances.
BREEDING: Egg-layer. Forms monogamous pairs that select a flat or vertical surface for spawning. Both parents fan and guard the eggs and defend the fry.
COMPATIBLE SPECIES: Peaceful tetras, corydoras, dwarf gouramis, and small catfish; avoid fin-nippers like tiger barbs and serpae tetras, and tiny fish such as neon tetras or guppy fry.
DIFFICULTY LEVEL: Moderate.
POPULARITY: Among the most recognized aquarium fish worldwide and a staple of freshwater displays.
NOTABLE FEATURES: Tall, laterally compressed body with extended dorsal and anal fins and a calm, regal motion, giving it a striking, angelic appearance.

Freshwater angelfish, *Pterophyllum scalare*. Copyright © Lochlainn Seabrook.

FRONTOSA CICHLID

AQUARIUM FISH PROFILE 17
COMMON NAME: Frontosa cichlid, blue variant.
SCIENTIFIC NAME: *Cyphotilapia frontosa*.
HABITAT TYPE: Freshwater; rocky shores of Lake Tanganyika.
ORIGIN: Northern Lake Tanganyika, East Africa.
SIZE: Up to 14 in TL.
LIFESPAN: 15–25 years.
COLORATION: The blue variant displays alternating vertical black bars over a pale to electric blue body. Males develop a pronounced cranial hump. Fins are often translucent blue with darker edging. Intensity of color varies with age, lighting, and dominance.
DIET: Carnivorous. Feeds on small fish, crustaceans, and invertebrates. In captivity accepts high-protein pellets, frozen krill, shrimp, and earthworms.
TEMPERAMENT: Generally peaceful for its size but territorial during breeding. Avoid small or aggressive tankmates.
TANK LEVEL: Middle to bottom.
MINIMUM TANK SIZE: 125 gal for a small group.
AQUARIUM CONDITIONS: Maintain at 74–80 °F, pH 8.0–9.0, hardness 10–20 dGH. Provide deep substrate of sand or fine gravel, large rocks, and caves to mimic rocky lake habitats. Strong filtration and moderate current required.
BEHAVIOR: Forms loose colonies. Swims slowly and deliberately. Prefers dim lighting and vertical rock formations. Sensitive to sudden movement or loud vibration.
BREEDING: Maternal mouthbrooder. Female carries up to 50 eggs in her mouth for 3–4 weeks. Fry emerge fully formed and are guarded for several days. Reproduction is slow; pairs form long-term bonds.
COMPATIBLE SPECIES: Other large, calm Tanganyikan cichlids such as featherfins or calvus. Should not be housed with aggressive or fin-nipping species such as tiger barbs or redtail sharks.
DIFFICULTY LEVEL: Moderate.
POPULARITY: Highly prized among advanced cichlid keepers worldwide for its size, intelligence, and striking appearance.
NOTABLE FEATURES: Distinctive forehead hump, long lifespan, and vivid blue bars make this one of the most recognizable African cichlids. Often serves as a centerpiece species in large display aquariums. Valued for its calm demeanor and majestic swimming behavior, reflecting the slow grandeur of its deep-lake origins and the quiet strength of Tanganyika's ancient ecosystem.

Frontosa cichlid (blue variant), *Cyphotilapia frontosa*. Copyright © Lochlainn Seabrook.

GARDNER'S KILLIFISH

AQUARIUM FISH PROFILE 18
COMMON NAME: Gardner's killifish.
SCIENTIFIC NAME: *Fundulopanchax gardneri*.
HABITAT TYPE: Freshwater; shallow forest pools and streams.
ORIGIN: Nigeria and Cameroon, in shaded rainforest pools, creeks, and slow-moving streams with dense vegetation and leaf litter.
SIZE: Reaches up to 2.5 in TL for males and about 2 in for females.
LIFESPAN: About 3 years in captivity with stable water quality and varied diet.
COLORATION: Males exhibit a turquoise-blue body with dense red spotting, yellow or orange edging on the dorsal, anal, and caudal fins, and iridescent highlights that intensify during courtship. Females are smaller, with subdued beige and brown tones and faint red markings.
DIET: Omnivorous; accepts small live or frozen foods such as daphnia, bloodworms, and brine shrimp. Will also eat quality flakes or micro-pellets.
TEMPERAMENT: Peaceful but territorial toward other males. Keep singly or one male with several females.
TANK LEVEL: Middle to top.
MINIMUM TANK SIZE: 10 gallons for a breeding trio or small colony.
AQUARIUM CONDITIONS: Temperature 72–77°F; pH 6.0–7.5; soft to moderately hard water; minimal flow. Provide floating plants, dim lighting, and a tight lid, as this species likes to jump.
BEHAVIOR: Energetic and alert, exploring all areas of the aquarium. Males display to females with flared fins and color changes.
BREEDING: Straightforward. Spawns in fine-leaved plants or synthetic mops. Eggs hatch in 10–14 days, depending on temperature. Fry accept infusoria or newly hatched brine shrimp. Adults may consume eggs, so separation is advised.
COMPATIBLE SPECIES: Peaceful community fish such as corydoras, neon tetras, harlequin rasboras, and small gouramis. Avoid fin-nippers like tiger barbs or serpae tetras.
DIFFICULTY LEVEL: Moderate.
POPULARITY: Common and well-established in the aquarium trade due to its beauty, small size, and ease of care.
NOTABLE FEATURES: Brilliantly patterned, sexually dimorphic African killifish noted for hardiness and prolific breeding in aquaria.

Gardner's killifish, *Fundulopanchax gardneri*. Copyright © Lochlainn Seabrook.

GERMAN BLUE RAM

AQUARIUM FISH PROFILE 19
COMMON NAME: German blue ram.
SCIENTIFIC NAME: *Mikrogeophagus ramirezi*.
HABITAT TYPE: Freshwater; warm, slow Orinoco Basin streams.
ORIGIN: Orinoco River basin, Venezuela and Colombia.
SIZE: Up to 2.5 in TL.
LIFESPAN: 2–4 years.
COLORATION: Iridescent blue scales over a golden-yellow body with a black vertical stripe through the eye, red-tipped dorsal and pelvic fins, and a bright red eye. Males show longer dorsal rays, broader bodies, and more intense coloration, while females develop a pink belly when ready to spawn.
DIET: Omnivore; accepts quality flakes, micro pellets, live, and frozen foods such as brine shrimp, daphnia, and bloodworms. Supplement with plant matter for best color and health.
TEMPERAMENT: Peaceful but territorial during spawning. Thrives in community aquariums with calm tankmates.
TANK LEVEL: Mid to bottom.
MINIMUM TANK SIZE: 20 gal for a pair; 30 gal or larger for a small group.
AQUARIUM CONDITIONS: Soft, slightly acidic water with stable parameters. Maintain 80–86 °F, pH 5.5–7.0, hardness below 10 dGH, and low nitrate levels. Provide a fine sand substrate, driftwood, caves, and dense plants for shelter.
BEHAVIOR: Active during the day; explores substrate and plants for food. Responds to human movement outside the tank. Prefers subdued lighting and quiet surroundings. Sensitive to ammonia and sudden temperature changes.
BREEDING: Biparental substrate spawner. Eggs laid on flat stones or leaves and guarded by both parents. Fry hatch in 2–3 days and become free-swimming in about a week.
COMPATIBLE SPECIES: Neon tetras, corydoras catfish, cardinal tetras, dwarf gouramis, and small rasboras. Avoid aggressive or fast species such as tiger barbs or redtail sharks.
DIFFICULTY LEVEL: Moderate; requires stable water quality and attentive care.
POPULARITY: One of the world's most admired dwarf cichlids, prized for its radiant colors and intelligent, interactive nature.
NOTABLE FEATURES: Displays true pair bonding, advanced parental care, and an unusually expressive range of behaviors for such a small fish, making it a centerpiece of planted aquariums.

German blue ram, *Mikrogeophagus ramirezi*. Copyright © Lochlainn Seabrook.

GLASS CATFISH

AQUARIUM FISH PROFILE 20
COMMON NAME: Glass catfish.
SCIENTIFIC NAME: *Kryptopterus vitreolus*.
HABITAT TYPE: Freshwater; clear, slow rivers and streams.
ORIGIN: Rivers and streams of central and southern Thailand.
SIZE: Up to 4 in TL.
LIFESPAN: 6–8 years in captivity.
COLORATION: Entirely transparent with a faint silver tint; internal organs and bones visible; fins delicate and almost invisible.
DIET: Omnivorous; eats live, frozen, and flake foods such as brine shrimp, bloodworms, and daphnia.
TEMPERAMENT: Peaceful schooling fish; shy when kept alone; thrives in groups of six or more.
TANK LEVEL: Midwater.
MINIMUM TANK SIZE: 30 gallons for a small group.
AQUARIUM CONDITIONS: Soft, slightly acidic water; 75–80 °F; pH 6.0–7.0; gentle filtration; subdued lighting; planted environment.
BEHAVIOR: Swims in coordinated groups; avoids bright light and turbulent water; easily stressed by loud sounds or sudden movement.
BREEDING: Rare in captivity; egg-scattering species; spawning occurs in dim light among fine plants; fry are delicate and difficult to raise.
COMPATIBLE SPECIES: Neon tetras, harlequin rasboras, corydoras catfish, and peaceful gouramis.
DIFFICULTY LEVEL: Moderate; sensitive to poor water quality or social isolation.
POPULARITY: High among aquarists for its unusual transparency and calm presence.
NOTABLE FEATURES: One of the few truly transparent vertebrates kept in aquariums; lacks scales and pigment; graceful and ghostlike when schooling; transparency serves as camouflage in clear water; best viewed under side lighting to reveal skeletal detail; visible heart motion adds to its scientific fascination; should always be kept in peaceful communities with low current; symbolizes precision and delicacy in advanced aquarium design; thrives when provided with gentle aeration and dense vegetation; exhibits schooling precision rivaling marine species; considered a living example of natural minimalism and evolutionary refinement, captivating aquarists and biologists alike.

Glass catfish, *Kryptopterus vitreolus*. Copyright © Lochlainn Seabrook.

GREEN MANDARIN DRAGONET

AQUARIUM FISH PROFILE 21
COMMON NAME: Green mandarin dragonet.
SCIENTIFIC NAME: *Synchiropus splendidus*.
HABITAT TYPE: Marine; warm sandy lagoons and coral reefs.
ORIGIN: Western Pacific Ocean, from the Philippines to Australia.
SIZE: Up to 3 in TL.
LIFESPAN: 10–15 years in ideal aquarium conditions.
COLORATION: Bright green body with vivid orange bars, blue facial stripes, and red highlights on fins. Males display a taller dorsal fin. Often described as the "living jewel of coral reefs."
DIET: Primarily live copepods, amphipods, and other small crustaceans. Supplemental feeding may include finely chopped frozen mysis or brine shrimp.
TEMPERAMENT: Peaceful and shy. Should not be housed with aggressive or fast-feeding species such as damselfish or six-line wrasse.
TANK LEVEL: Bottom to mid-level.
MINIMUM TANK SIZE: 30 gallons for a single specimen with a mature live rock system.
AQUARIUM CONDITIONS: Temperature 75–82°F, pH 8.1–8.4, salinity 1.020–1.025, stable reef setup with live rock and sand substrate.
BEHAVIOR: Moves gracefully across the substrate, picking at microfauna throughout the day. Often rests on the sand or rock ledges using its pelvic fins.
BREEDING: Pair-spawning occurs at dusk; the male and female rise together, releasing eggs and sperm into the water column. Larvae are planktonic and require specialized feeding.
COMPATIBLE SPECIES: Peaceful tankmates such as gobies, clownfish, firefish, and small cardinalfish. Avoid aggressive feeders like dottybacks or wrasses.
DIFFICULTY LEVEL: Moderate to advanced due to specialized diet and habitat needs. Requires an established copepod population for long-term survival in captivity. Best maintained in mature reef systems with minimal competition for food.
POPULARITY: Iconic reef species favored for its brilliant coloration and gentle nature. Widely admired by marine hobbyists and photographers.
NOTABLE FEATURES: Known for its psychedelic patterning and slow, hovering movement; among the most visually distinctive and photographed fish in the marine aquarium hobby.

Green mandarin dragonet, *Synchiropus splendidus*. Copyright © Lochlainn Seabrook.

HARLEQUIN RASBORA

AQUARIUM FISH PROFILE 22
COMMON NAME: Harlequin rasbora.
SCIENTIFIC NAME: *Trigonostigma heteromorpha*.
HABITAT TYPE: Freshwater; shaded peat swamps and streams.
ORIGIN: Thailand, Malaysia, Singapore, and Sumatra.
SIZE: Up to 2 in TL.
LIFESPAN: About 5 to 8 years.
COLORATION: Metallic orange-pink body with a distinctive black triangular patch extending from mid-body to tail; males are more vividly colored and slender.
DIET: Omnivore; consumes fine flake food, micro pellets, daphnia, and brine shrimp.
TEMPERAMENT: Peaceful schooling fish; thrives in calm community tanks.
TANK LEVEL: Middle to upper.
MINIMUM TANK SIZE: 15 gallons for a small group.
AQUARIUM CONDITIONS: Temperature 72–82°F; pH 6.0–7.5; soft, slightly acidic water with dense vegetation and subdued lighting.
BEHAVIOR: Active midwater swimmer; prefers to be in groups of six or more; displays schooling cohesion and synchronized turns.
BREEDING: Egg-scattering species; pairs spawn beneath broad leaves such as those of Cryptocoryne; fry hatch within 24 hours and require infusoria or liquid fry food.
COMPATIBLE SPECIES: Neon tetras, corydoras catfish, and small gouramis.
DIFFICULTY LEVEL: Easy to moderate; tolerant of a range of water parameters but requires stable, clean water.
POPULARITY: Very popular; one of the most common and enduring community fish species in home aquariums.
NOTABLE FEATURES: Recognized for its striking triangular flank marking and fluid schooling motion; adapted to calm, shaded forest streams. Its reflective scales shimmer under aquarium light, producing a warm copper glow. Harlequins are often used as visual balance fish in planted aquascapes due to their contrast and steady motion. They benefit from tannin-rich environments created by driftwood or leaf litter. Well-fed individuals exhibit enhanced coloration and longevity. In nature they inhabit peat swamps, blackwater pools, and shaded forest creeks where light penetration is minimal. Their stability and color make them ideal reference fish for observing environmental changes in established aquaria.

Harlequin rasbora, *Trigonostigma heteromorpha*. Copyright © Lochlainn Seabrook.

JACK DEMPSEY

AQUARIUM FISH PROFILE 23
COMMON NAME: Jack Dempsey.
SCIENTIFIC NAME: *Rocio octofasciata*.
HABITAT TYPE: Freshwater; warm, slow rivers and lagoons.
ORIGIN: Central America, from southern Mexico to Honduras.
SIZE: Up to 10 in TL.
LIFESPAN: 8–10 years.
COLORATION: Base color dark brown to gray with iridescent blue-green and gold spangling; males develop brighter metallic hues and elongated fins, while females remain smaller and less vivid. Juveniles are paler with faint barring.
DIET: Omnivore; accepts flakes, pellets, live, and frozen foods including worms, insects, and crustaceans.
TEMPERAMENT: Territorial and aggressive, especially during breeding; best kept singly or in large tanks with other robust cichlids.
TANK LEVEL: Middle to bottom.
MINIMUM TANK SIZE: 55 gal.
AQUARIUM CONDITIONS: Temperature 72–82°F; pH 6.5–8.0; moderate hardness; provide sand substrate, caves, and rocky cover with open swimming space.
BEHAVIOR: Intelligent and interactive; may rearrange décor and dig substrate; will display vivid colors when excited or defending territory.
BREEDING: Substrate spawner; forms monogamous pairs; both parents guard eggs and fry; high parental care. Incubation lasts about three days, with free-swimming fry in one week.
COMPATIBLE SPECIES: Other large Central American cichlids like oscars or firemouths if tank is spacious; catfish or plecos may also coexist. Avoid pairing with peaceful species such as angelfish or tetras.
DIFFICULTY LEVEL: Moderate.
POPULARITY: Common.
NOTABLE FEATURES: Named after the famous 20th-Century boxer due to its bold attitude. Known for vibrant coloration, strong personality, and long history as a classic aquarium species. Recognized for its adaptability and ability to thrive in a wide range of water conditions. A favorite among aquarists for over 100 years and still regarded as a symbol of the hardy Central American cichlid group. Its color intensity changes with mood, dominance, and breeding activity.

Jack Dempsey, *Rocio octofasciata*. Copyright © Lochlainn Seabrook.

KISSING GOURAMI

AQUARIUM FISH PROFILE 24
COMMON NAME: Kissing gourami.
SCIENTIFIC NAME: *Helostoma temminckii*.
HABITAT TYPE: Freshwater; slow, vegetated lakes and rivers.
ORIGIN: Thailand, Cambodia, Malaysia, and Indonesia.
SIZE: Up to 12 in TL.
LIFESPAN: 10–15 years in captivity.
COLORATION: Pale pink, green, or silvery with faint iridescent tones; body tall and laterally compressed; lips thick and fleshy, equipped with fine tooth plates for scraping algae and biofilm.
DIET: Omnivorous; consumes algae, detritus, soft plants, and small invertebrates; thrives on flakes, pellets, blanched vegetables, and live or frozen foods such as brine shrimp and bloodworms.
TEMPERAMENT: Peaceful toward most species, but males engage in ritualized "kissing" contests to establish social order; these displays rarely cause injury.
TANK LEVEL: Mid to top.
MINIMUM TANK SIZE: 55 gallons for one or two adults with open swimming space and surface access.
AQUARIUM CONDITIONS: 75–82 °F; pH 6.5–7.5; moderate hardness; subdued lighting; dense vegetation and floating plants provide shade and security; use gentle filtration and regular water changes.
BEHAVIOR: Active, calm, and hardy; spends much of the day grazing on algae and plant surfaces; avoid aggressive fin-nippers such as tiger barbs and redtail sharks.
BREEDING: Egg scatterer; spawns beneath floating vegetation; eggs hatch in 24–36 hours; fry are free-swimming by day three and require infusoria before transitioning to finely crushed flake.
COMPATIBLE SPECIES: Angelfish, pearl gouramis, rainbowfish, larger rasboras, danios, and peaceful catfish.
DIFFICULTY LEVEL: Easy.
POPULARITY: Among the most recognizable gouramis in the aquarium trade; valued for its resilience, distinctive appearance, and longevity.
NOTABLE FEATURES: Possesses a labyrinth organ that allows breathing of atmospheric air; uses its fleshy lips both for grazing and for dominance display; graceful, slow-moving, and capable of adapting to varied environments; displays striking reflective highlights under aquarium lighting, accentuating its elegance and calm demeanor.

Kissing gourami, *Helostoma temminckii*. Copyright © Lochlainn Seabrook.

LINED SEAHORSE

AQUARIUM FISH PROFILE 25
COMMON NAME: Lined seahorse.
SCIENTIFIC NAME: *Hippocampus erectus*.
HABITAT TYPE: Marine; warm seagrass beds and coastal reefs.
ORIGIN: Western Atlantic Ocean from Nova Scotia to Argentina, including the Gulf of Mexico and Caribbean Sea.
SIZE: Up to 7 in TL.
LIFESPAN: 4–6 years in captivity under optimal care.
COLORATION: Varies from yellow, orange, brown, gray, or black with fine white lines or spots; color may change to match surroundings or mood.
DIET: Carnivorous; feeds on live or frozen mysid shrimp, copepods, and small crustaceans.
TEMPERAMENT: Peaceful and slow-moving; best kept with calm, non-aggressive tankmates.
TANK LEVEL: Mid to lower regions, often clinging to plants, coral, or decor with prehensile tail.
MINIMUM TANK SIZE: 30 gallons for a pair.
AQUARIUM CONDITIONS: Temperature 72–77°F; salinity 1.020–1.025; pH 8.1–8.4; gentle water flow with vertical space for courtship and swimming.
BEHAVIOR: Diurnal and highly social; forms strong pair bonds and engages in daily greeting rituals; poor swimmers relying on dorsal fin propulsion.
BREEDING: Ovoviviparous; males carry eggs in a ventral brood pouch for about 20 days before giving birth to up to 200 young.
COMPATIBLE SPECIES: Ideal companions include pipefish and small gobies; avoid fin-nippers such as tiger barbs or sergeant majors.
DIFFICULTY LEVEL: Moderate to high; requires stable water quality and live foods for optimal health.
POPULARITY: Highly sought after for marine display tanks due to its graceful appearance and unique reproductive habits.
NOTABLE FEATURES: One of the largest seahorse species; exhibits monogamous pair bonding and paternal brooding; able to change color for camouflage or communication. Its eyes move independently, allowing simultaneous forward and backward vision. Possesses bony plates instead of scales, providing natural armor against predators. Moves by rapid oscillation of the dorsal fin and can anchor itself securely during currents with its strong, curling tail.

Lined seahorse, *Hippocampus erectus*. Copyright © Lochlainn Seabrook.

LIONFISH

AQUARIUM FISH PROFILE 26
COMMON NAME: Lionfish.
SCIENTIFIC NAME: *Pterois volitans*.
HABITAT TYPE: Marine; tropical coral reefs and rocky ledges.
ORIGIN: Indo-Pacific region, from the Red Sea and East Africa to Australia and Japan.
SIZE: Up to 15 in TL; weight up to 2.6 lb.
LIFESPAN: 10–15 years in captivity.
COLORATION: Alternating vertical bands of reddish-brown and white; long, fanlike pectoral fins and tall dorsal spines that form a striking display.
DIET: Carnivorous; feeds on small fish, shrimp, and crustaceans. Accepts frozen or live foods such as silversides and mysis shrimp in captivity.
TEMPERAMENT: Aggressive predator but generally ignores non-prey species. Venomous spines require careful handling.
TANK LEVEL: Mid to bottom.
MINIMUM TANK SIZE: 120 gal for adults.
AQUARIUM CONDITIONS: Temperature 75–82°F; salinity 1.020–1.025; pH 8.1–8.4; strong filtration and moderate water movement.
BEHAVIOR: Slow-moving ambush hunter; hovers motionless before lunging at prey. Spines contain venom used for defense. Active mainly at night. Often rests inverted beneath ledges or within coral structures during the day.
BREEDING: Difficult in captivity. Males court females with display dances; eggs are released in gelatinous masses that float near the surface.
COMPATIBLE SPECIES: Best with large, non-aggressive tankmates such as groupers or tangs. Avoid fin-nippers like sergeant majors or clown triggers.
DIFFICULTY LEVEL: Moderate; requires space, careful feeding, and attention to tankmates.
POPULARITY: Highly popular among advanced marine aquarists for its beauty and dramatic appearance.
NOTABLE FEATURES: Possesses up to 18 venomous spines. Introduced populations in the Atlantic have become invasive due to rapid reproduction and lack of predators. Its graceful fins and vivid stripes make it one of the most photographed marine aquarium species. Admired for both its elegance and quiet dominance in the reef environment.

Lionfish, *Pterois volitans*. Copyright © Lochlainn Seabrook.

MOORISH IDOL

AQUARIUM FISH PROFILE 27
COMMON NAME: Moorish idol.
SCIENTIFIC NAME: *Zanclus cornutus*.
HABITAT TYPE: Marine; tropical coral reefs and warm reef flats.
ORIGIN: Indo-Pacific region, from East Africa and the Red Sea to Hawaii, southern Japan, and the Great Barrier Reef.
SIZE: Up to 9 in TL.
LIFESPAN: Typically 5–7 years in captivity; shorter under stress.
COLORATION: Striking white body with two wide black vertical bands and a bright yellow band across the midsection; tail yellow, snout narrow and elongated; dorsal fin extends into a long trailing filament.
DIET: Omnivore; eats sponges, tunicates, coral polyps, filamentous algae, and small benthic invertebrates; in captivity accepts sponge-based frozen foods, mysis shrimp, and marine algae.
TEMPERAMENT: Peaceful but delicate; easily frightened by aggressive or fast-moving species.
TANK LEVEL: Mid to upper.
MINIMUM TANK SIZE: 180 gal.
AQUARIUM CONDITIONS: Temperature 75–82°F; pH 8.1–8.4; salinity 1.020–1.025; requires strong current, pristine water, and ample live rock for constant grazing.
BEHAVIOR: Persistent forager that swims gracefully in open water; often rests among rock crevices; thrives in calm, stable surroundings; may nip at corals if underfed.
BREEDING: Not achieved in captivity; wild pairs release pelagic eggs that hatch into long transparent larvae called acronurus, which drift before settling.
COMPATIBLE SPECIES: Best kept with gentle marine fish such as tangs, gobies, or clownfish; avoid triggers or large angelfish that cause stress.
DIFFICULTY LEVEL: Extremely high; prone to starvation and stress; recommended only for expert aquarists.
POPULARITY: Iconic and admired worldwide for beauty and symbolism; featured on marine logos, artwork, and stamps.
NOTABLE FEATURES: Laterally compressed body, tubular snout, trailing dorsal streamer, and continuous fin motion; often mistaken for butterflyfish though the only living member of its family, Zanclidae, and a true symbol of tropical reef elegance; its graceful presence makes it a centerpiece of large public aquariums and underwater photography.

Moorish idol, *Zanclus cornutus*. Copyright © Lochlainn Seabrook.

OCELLARIS CLOWNFISH

AQUARIUM FISH PROFILE 28
COMMON NAME: Ocellaris clownfish.
SCIENTIFIC NAME: *Amphiprion ocellaris*.
HABITAT TYPE: Marine; shallow coral reefs and warm lagoons.
ORIGIN: Indo-Pacific region, from the eastern Indian Ocean to northwestern Australia and the Philippines.
SIZE: Up to 4.3 in TL.
LIFESPAN: 6–10 years in captivity, occasionally longer.
COLORATION: Bright orange body with three vertical white bars outlined in black. Fins bordered in black. Color intensity varies with diet, health, mood, and lighting.
DIET: Omnivorous. Eats zooplankton, small crustaceans, and algae. In aquariums, accepts pellets, frozen foods, and finely chopped seafood.
TEMPERAMENT: Peaceful and social but may defend its host anemone. Suitable for community tanks if space is adequate.
TANK LEVEL: Mid to lower levels, near host anemones or coral structures.
MINIMUM TANK SIZE: 20 gallons for a pair.
AQUARIUM CONDITIONS: Temperature 74–82°F, pH 8.0–8.4, salinity 1.020–1.025. Requires stable water quality and moderate current.
BEHAVIOR: Slow, deliberate swimmer. Forms symbiotic relationships with sea anemones such as *Heteractis magnifica* and *Stichodactyla gigantea*. Exhibits natural hierarchy with a dominant female and smaller males.
BREEDING: Egg layer. Pairs form long-term bonds. Female deposits eggs near the anemone base; male guards and fans them until hatching after 6–8 days.
COMPATIBLE SPECIES: Peaceful reef fish such as gobies, blennies, and cardinalfish. Avoid aggressive species like damselfish and dottybacks.
DIFFICULTY LEVEL: Easy to moderate. Hardy once acclimated and adapts well to captive conditions.
POPULARITY: Iconic. One of the most recognized and frequently kept marine fish worldwide.
NOTABLE FEATURES: Known for its mutualistic relationship with sea anemones, immune to their stings through a protective mucous coating. Thrives in pairs or small groups when introduced carefully. Distinguishable from the similar *Amphiprion percula* by its thinner black margins.

Clownfish, ocellaris, *Amphiprion ocellaris*. Copyright © Lochlainn Seabrook.

OSCAR

AQUARIUM FISH PROFILE 29
COMMON NAME: Oscar.
SCIENTIFIC NAME: *Astronotus ocellatus*.
HABITAT TYPE: Freshwater; slow Amazon rivers and floodplains.
ORIGIN: Amazon River basin, South America.
SIZE: Up to 14 in TL; average adult 10–12 in; 2–3 lb.
LIFESPAN: 10–15 years.
COLORATION: Base color olive to dark brown with orange, red, or gold patterning; domesticated varieties include tiger, albino, and lemon forms. Fins broad and rounded, often rimmed in orange or red. Eyes large with red or orange irises.
DIET: Omnivorous; accepts pellets, shrimp, fish, worms, and vegetables. Requires varied high-protein diet to maintain color and health.
TEMPERAMENT: Intelligent, territorial, and semi-aggressive, especially toward smaller or similar-sized fish. Best kept singly or in pairs.
TANK LEVEL: Primarily mid to bottom.
MINIMUM TANK SIZE: 75 gallons for one adult; larger for pairs.
AQUARIUM CONDITIONS: Temperature 74–82°F; pH 6.0–7.5; soft to moderately hard water. Provide strong filtration, open swimming space, and sturdy decorations.
BEHAVIOR: Recognizes owners, can be hand-fed, and displays curiosity. May rearrange substrate and decorations. Territorial during feeding and breeding.
BREEDING: Biparental egg-layer; forms monogamous pairs. Spawns on flat surfaces; both parents guard eggs and fry.
COMPATIBLE SPECIES: Large, robust fish such as silver dollars or plecostomus. Avoid fin-nippers like tiger barbs or aggressive cichlids such as jack dempseys.
DIFFICULTY LEVEL: Moderate.
POPULARITY: Highly popular for personality, coloration, and interactivity.
NOTABLE FEATURES: Intelligent, responsive fish known for recognizing human caretakers; displays strong pair bonds and complex behaviors rare among aquarium species. Commonly seen as a centerpiece fish in large tropical aquariums. Requires stable conditions and attentive care to thrive. Considered one of the most personable and trainable aquarium species. In well-kept tanks, individuals often live beyond 15 years and exhibit distinctive learned behaviors unique to each specimen.

Oscar, *Astronotus ocellatus*. Copyright © Lochlainn Seabrook.

PAJAMA CARDINALFISH

AQUARIUM FISH PROFILE 30
COMMON NAME: Pajama cardinalfish.
SCIENTIFIC NAME: *Sphaeramia nematoptera*.
HABITAT TYPE: Marine; shallow coastal reefs, tropical lagoons, and warm sheltered bays.
ORIGIN: Western Pacific Ocean, from the Philippines to Fiji.
SIZE: Up to 3 in TL.
LIFESPAN: 5 years on average.
COLORATION: The head and anterior body are bright yellow to golden, transitioning into a dark vertical mid-body band followed by a whitish rear section covered with reddish-orange spots (hence its common name). The eyes are vivid red-orange, and the fins are translucent with yellow and orange highlights.
DIET: Carnivorous; feeds on plankton, small crustaceans, and meaty prepared foods.
TEMPERAMENT: Peaceful, schooling species; best kept in small groups. Avoid aggressive fish such as tiger barbs or redtail sharks.
TANK LEVEL: Mid to upper levels.
MINIMUM TANK SIZE: 30 gallons for a small group.
AQUARIUM CONDITIONS: Temperature 74–80°F; pH 8.1–8.4; specific gravity 1.020–1.025; moderate flow; well-oxygenated, stable reef system with live rock and shaded areas.
BEHAVIOR: Slow-moving, nocturnally active fish that hovers near rock crevices. Remains calm when threatened and seeks refuge among coral branches.
BREEDING: Mouthbrooding species. The male carries eggs in his mouth until hatching. Spawns readily in captivity when kept in stable pairs.
COMPATIBLE SPECIES: Clownfish, gobies, firefish, and peaceful tangs. Shows mild territorial behavior toward similar species when overcrowded.
DIFFICULTY LEVEL: Easy to moderate.
POPULARITY: Common in the aquarium trade due to its striking coloration and hardy nature.
NOTABLE FEATURES: Unique polka-dot body pattern and contrasting band make it instantly recognizable. Displays strong pair bonding and cooperative group behavior. Adaptable to both reef and fish-only tanks. Excellent beginner choice for peaceful community aquariums. Thrives in dim lighting; often hovers motionless, creating a calm visual centerpiece in the tank. Highly social and best maintained in small groups to reduce stress.

Pajama cardinalfish, *Sphaeramia nematoptera*. Copyright © Lochlainn Seabrook.

PEARL GOURAMI

AQUARIUM FISH PROFILE 31
COMMON NAME: Pearl gourami.
SCIENTIFIC NAME: *Trichopodus leerii*.
HABITAT TYPE: Freshwater; calm, weedy swamps and streams.
ORIGIN: Slow-moving, vegetation-rich waters of Thailand, Malaysia, Indonesia, and Borneo.
SIZE: Up to 5 in TL.
LIFESPAN: 5–7 years.
COLORATION: Silvery white body covered with pearly spots; a distinct black horizontal stripe runs from the mouth through the tail base; fins often edged with orange or red in males, which also develop reddish-orange breasts during breeding.
DIET: Omnivorous; consumes flakes, pellets, live and frozen foods such as bloodworms, daphnia, and brine shrimp.
TEMPERAMENT: Peaceful, shy; best in calm community tanks.
TANK LEVEL: Middle to upper regions.
MINIMUM TANK SIZE: 30 gallons.
AQUARIUM CONDITIONS: Temperature 77–82°F; pH 6.0–8.0; soft to moderately hard water; low to moderate current with dense floating vegetation for shade and bubble-nest construction.
BEHAVIOR: Gentle schooling species preferring groups of five or more; uses its labyrinth organ to gulp air at the surface; glides slowly among plants.
BREEDING: Bubble-nest builder; male constructs a floating nest of bubbles beneath leaves, then guards eggs and fry; requires shallow, warm, well-covered breeding tank.
COMPATIBLE SPECIES: Neon tetra, harlequin rasbora, corydoras catfish, cherry barb, and other peaceful community fish. Avoid housing with aggressive or fin-nipping fish such as tiger barbs or red-tailed sharks.
DIFFICULTY LEVEL: Easy to moderate.
POPULARITY: Highly popular for its beauty, hardiness, and graceful behavior; a staple in freshwater aquaria worldwide.
NOTABLE FEATURES: Possesses a labyrinth organ allowing direct air breathing; known for its reflective "pearl" patterning and tranquil nature. A symbol of calm and elegance in community tanks. Thrives in dim lighting that enhances its iridescent scales. Best kept with soft substrate and subdued filtration to mimic its native still waters. Prefers well-established aquariums with stable, clean water conditions and abundant plant cover. Often serves as a visual centerpiece in peaceful tropical aquariums.

Pearl gourami, *Trichopodus leerii*. Copyright © Lochlainn Seabrook.

PICASSO TRIGGERFISH

AQUARIUM FISH PROFILE 32
COMMON NAME: Picasso triggerfish.
SCIENTIFIC NAME: *Rhinecanthus aculeatus*.
HABITAT TYPE: Marine; tropical shallow reef flats, warm sandy lagoons, and seaward reef slopes with coral rubble.
ORIGIN: Indo-Pacific region, from the Red Sea and East Africa to the Hawaiian Islands.
SIZE: Reaches up to 10 in TL and 2 lb.
LIFESPAN: Commonly 10 years, occasionally exceeding 12 under ideal care.
COLORATION: Cream to light tan body marked with bold blue, yellow, and black diagonal lines. Distinct blue streaks cross the snout and eyes; tail fin pale with dark edging.
DIET: Omnivorous; feeds on crustaceans, worms, small fish, and filamentous algae. Must be offered meaty frozen foods, clams, shrimp, squid, and quality marine pellets.
TEMPERAMENT: Assertive, intelligent, and highly territorial, particularly toward similar-shaped or smaller fish. Keep singly or with large, robust species only.
TANK LEVEL: Mid to bottom zones, frequently sifting sand for prey.
MINIMUM TANK SIZE: 75 gallons for juveniles; 120 gallons or larger for adults.
AQUARIUM CONDITIONS: Temperature 75–82°F; pH 8.1–8.4; salinity 1.020–1.025; strong filtration and moderate water flow; secure lid required to prevent jumping.
BEHAVIOR: Active diurnal forager; uses its mouth to move sand, stones, and shells; may vocalize with grunting or clicking sounds when alarmed or handled.
BREEDING: Oviparous; forms monogamous pairs; eggs laid in sandy depressions guarded by both parents until hatching.
COMPATIBLE SPECIES: Large tangs, wrasses, puffers, and groupers. Avoid housing with small gobies, blennies, or damselfish.
DIFFICULTY LEVEL: Intermediate; requires marine experience and strict attention to water quality.
POPULARITY: Among the most recognized and photographed triggerfish in the aquarium trade.
NOTABLE FEATURES: Possesses a dorsal trigger spine for defense; can wedge itself securely in rock crevices; complex color pattern gives it a painterly, abstract appearance that inspired its common name.

Picasso triggerfish, *Rhinecanthus aculeatus*. Copyright © Lochlainn Seabrook.

POWDER BLUE TANG

AQUARIUM FISH PROFILE 33
COMMON NAME: Powder blue tang.
SCIENTIFIC NAME: *Acanthurus leucosternon*.
HABITAT TYPE: Marine; tropical coral reefs and clear lagoons.
ORIGIN: Indian Ocean, from East Africa to the Maldives and Sri Lanka, extending east to the Andaman Sea.
SIZE: Up to 9 in TL.
LIFESPAN: 10–15 years in captivity with proper care.
COLORATION: Body bright azure-blue with a black face mask, white chest, and vivid yellow dorsal fin; pectoral and pelvic fins pale blue to white; tail edged in black.
DIET: Primarily herbivorous, grazing on filamentous algae; supplements include nori, spirulina, and marine vegetable blends.
TEMPERAMENT: Semi-aggressive; territorial toward similar-shaped tangs or other surgeonfish.
TANK LEVEL: Midwater swimmer.
MINIMUM TANK SIZE: 125 gal for a single adult.
AQUARIUM CONDITIONS: Temperature 75–82°F; pH 8.1–8.4; salinity 1.020–1.025; strong current and high oxygenation required.
BEHAVIOR: Constant grazer and fast swimmer reaching brief speeds of 5 mph; may chase intruders near feeding areas.
BREEDING: Rare in captivity; pelagic spawner releasing eggs and sperm into open water at dusk.
COMPATIBLE SPECIES: Peaceful fish such as clownfish, chromis, and wrasses; avoid triggerfish or other tangs.
DIFFICULTY LEVEL: Intermediate to advanced; requires pristine water and daily feeding to prevent disease.
POPULARITY: Very popular for its intense colors and graceful movement.
NOTABLE FEATURES: Scalpel-like spine at tail base used for defense; iconic blue body and yellow fin contrast. Commonly kept as a single specimen to avoid aggression. Needs large open areas for continuous swimming. Prone to stress-related marine ich if water quality declines. Sensitive to sudden environmental changes and low oxygen levels. Requires ample live rock for grazing and security. Benefits from ultraviolet sterilization to reduce parasite risk. Exhibits intelligent behavior and recognizes regular caretakers. Displays dominant body posturing during territorial displays but rarely inflicts injury. Thrives in reef setups with balanced light cycles and strong surface agitation.

Powder blue tang, *Acanthurus leucosternon*. Copyright © Lochlainn Seabrook.

PURPLE TANG

AQUARIUM FISH PROFILE 34
COMMON NAME: Purple tang.
SCIENTIFIC NAME: *Zebrasoma xanthurum*.
HABITAT TYPE: Marine; tropical coral reefs and rocky slopes.
ORIGIN: Red Sea and western Indian Ocean, especially around the Arabian Peninsula and Gulf of Aden.
SIZE: Up to 10 in TL.
LIFESPAN: Up to 30 years in captivity.
COLORATION: Deep violet-blue body with darker radiating lines and lighter shading on the face. Tail bright yellow, contrasting sharply with the body. Dorsal and anal fins edged in black. Color intensity deepens with maturity, health, and lighting.
DIET: Primarily herbivorous. Consumes algae, seaweed, nori, and spirulina. Accepts plant-based pellets and mysis shrimp. Requires daily vegetable matter to maintain coloration and immunity.
TEMPERAMENT: Generally peaceful but territorial toward similar tangs.
TANK LEVEL: Active in the middle and upper levels.
MINIMUM TANK SIZE: 125 gallons.
AQUARIUM CONDITIONS: Temperature 75–82°F. pH 8.1–8.4. Specific gravity 1.020–1.025. Requires strong flow, live rock, and high oxygen levels. Stable salinity is essential for long-term health.
BEHAVIOR: Constant grazer. Spends most of the day feeding on algae-coated surfaces. Displays brief circling or fin flaring when asserting dominance. Highly alert and quick to retreat into rockwork if startled. Frequently follows tank walls in repetitive swimming patterns.
BREEDING: Rare in captivity. In the wild, group spawning occurs near dusk with eggs released into open water. Larvae drift pelagically before settling among reef structures.
COMPATIBLE SPECIES: Clownfish, gobies, cardinalfish, and peaceful wrasses. Avoid housing with yellow tangs or sailfin tangs. Can coexist well with most peaceful reef fish when given ample space.
DIFFICULTY LEVEL: Moderate. Requires stable parameters and plentiful algae growth. Best maintained by experienced marine keepers.
POPULARITY: Very high among reef keepers for its vivid color and algae control.
NOTABLE FEATURES: Bright yellow tail and scalpel-like caudal spines used defensively.

Purple tang, *Zebrasoma xanthurum*. Copyright © Lochlainn Seabrook.

QUEEN ANGELFISH

AQUARIUM FISH PROFILE 35
COMMON NAME: Queen angelfish.
SCIENTIFIC NAME: *Holacanthus ciliaris*.
HABITAT TYPE: Marine; tropical coral reefs and warm reef edges.
ORIGIN: Western Atlantic, from Bermuda and Florida to Brazil, including the Caribbean and Gulf of Mexico.
SIZE: Up to 18 in TL; average 12 in in captivity.
LIFESPAN: 15 years or more with proper care.
COLORATION: Brilliant blue body with yellow fins and tail. Face marked with blue highlights. Crown-like blue patch edged in bright blue above the head gives the species its name. Juveniles show vertical blue and yellow bars that fade as they mature.
DIET: Omnivore. Feeds on sponges, algae, tunicates, and small invertebrates. In aquariums accepts marine angelfish preparations, mysis shrimp, and spirulina.
TEMPERAMENT: Semi-aggressive. Territorial toward other angelfish. Avoid housing with aggressive species such as triggerfish or large wrasses.
TANK LEVEL: Mid to upper.
MINIMUM TANK SIZE: 180 gal for adults.
AQUARIUM CONDITIONS: Temperature 72–82°F. pH 8.1–8.4. Salinity 1.020–1.025. Requires live rock for grazing and hiding.
BEHAVIOR: Active, alert, and intelligent. Spends much time grazing on rock surfaces. May form pairs or small groups in large systems. Swims with graceful, deliberate movements.
BREEDING: Difficult in captivity. In the wild spawns in pairs near dusk, releasing floating eggs. Larvae are planktonic for several weeks.
COMPATIBLE SPECIES: Peaceful tankmates such as tangs, clownfish, or gobies. Avoid aggressive or nipping species.
DIFFICULTY LEVEL: Moderate to challenging. Requires stable water quality and experienced care.
POPULARITY: Highly sought-after show fish among marine aquarists. Appreciated for its regal appearance and brilliant coloring.
NOTABLE FEATURES: Distinctive "queen's crown" on forehead. Vibrant blue and yellow contrast makes it one of the most iconic reef angelfish in the world. Its intelligence and striking beauty make it a centerpiece species in display aquariums. In the wild it helps maintain coral health by controlling sponge growth. Thrives best in large, well-established reef systems.

Queen angelfish, *Holacanthus ciliaris*. Copyright © Lochlainn Seabrook.

RACCOON BUTTERFLYFISH

AQUARIUM FISH PROFILE 36
COMMON NAME: Raccoon butterflyfish.
SCIENTIFIC NAME: *Chaetodon lunula*.
HABITAT TYPE: Marine; shallow coral reefs and warm reef flats.
ORIGIN: Indo-Pacific region, from Hawaii and Polynesia westward to the Indian Ocean and Red Sea.
SIZE: Up to 8 in TL.
LIFESPAN: Typically 5–7 years in captivity; up to 10 years in the wild.
COLORATION: Bright yellow body with a dark vertical mask across the eyes, a broad black band through the rear body and dorsal fin, and faint diagonal lines across the flanks. Fins edged in orange and white.
DIET: Omnivorous; consumes coral polyps, small crustaceans, worms, and algae. In aquariums, accepts mysis shrimp, brine shrimp, and prepared marine diets with vegetable matter.
TEMPERAMENT: Generally peaceful but may quarrel with other butterflyfish or similar-shaped species. Best kept singly or as a mated pair.
TANK LEVEL: Mid to upper levels.
MINIMUM TANK SIZE: 120 gal for adult specimens.
AQUARIUM CONDITIONS: Marine; temperature 74–82 °F, pH 8.1–8.4, specific gravity 1.020–1.025, moderate to strong water movement, live rock for grazing.
BEHAVIOR: Active diurnal swimmer; shelters among corals or rocks at night. Requires stable water quality and hiding spaces. May pick at sessile invertebrates.
BREEDING: Oviparous; forms monogamous pairs. Spawning occurs near dusk with eggs released into open water. Rarely achieved in captivity.
COMPATIBLE SPECIES: Peaceful reef fish such as tangs, wrasses, and gobies. Avoid aggressive species like triggers or large angelfish.
DIFFICULTY LEVEL: Moderate; needs experienced care and mature reef systems.
POPULARITY: Highly sought after for its striking coloration and graceful swimming behavior. Common in marine exhibits worldwide.
NOTABLE FEATURES: Distinct "raccoon" facial banding and thread-like dorsal fin rays make it instantly recognizable among butterflyfish. Also known for its adaptability across wide Indo-Pacific habitats.

Raccoon butterflyfish, *Chaetodon lunula*. Copyright © Lochlainn Seabrook.

RED LINE TORPEDO BARB

AQUARIUM FISH PROFILE 37
COMMON NAME: Red line torpedo barb.
SCIENTIFIC NAME: *Sahyadria denisonii*.
HABITAT TYPE: Freshwater; clear, fast hill streams and rivers.
ORIGIN: Hill streams and rivers of the Western Ghats, southern India.
SIZE: Up to 6 in TL.
LIFESPAN: 5 to 8 years.
COLORATION: Metallic silver body with a black lateral stripe running from snout through the tail, bordered above by a vivid red stripe that fades near the dorsal fin. The tail fin shows yellow and black bands, with color intensity strongest in active males.
DIET: Omnivorous; accepts flakes, pellets, frozen, and live foods such as brine shrimp and bloodworms.
TEMPERAMENT: Peaceful schooling fish that must be kept in groups of six or more.
TANK LEVEL: Mid to upper levels.
MINIMUM TANK SIZE: 55 gallons.
AQUARIUM CONDITIONS: Temperature 72–79°F; pH 6.5–7.5; moderate hardness; strong filtration and oxygenation with steady water movement.
BEHAVIOR: Active, fast-swimming, and coordinated. Enjoys open areas with shaded zones and vegetation for security. Displays intricate group turns and parallel swimming when relaxed. Often patrols the entire length of the aquarium in synchronized bursts.
BREEDING: Rare in home aquariums; spawning occurs in groups with eggs scattered among fine plants. Captive breeding success has been limited but is improving in controlled aquaculture. Males develop deeper coloration during courtship displays.
COMPATIBLE SPECIES: Best with peaceful community fish such as danios, rasboras, rainbowfish, and non-aggressive barbs. Avoid fin-nippers like tiger barbs and serpae tetras.
DIFFICULTY LEVEL: Moderate.
POPULARITY: Highly popular and prized for its beauty and motion. Commonly featured in public aquariums and advanced hobbyist tanks.
NOTABLE FEATURES: Endemic to India and threatened in the wild by habitat loss and overcollection. Known for its sleek shape and bright red stripe, giving it a torpedo-like appearance. Its streamlined form allows bursts of speed exceeding 6 mph. It is one of the most graceful and elegant freshwater fish ever discovered.

Red line torpedo barb, *Sahyadria denisonii*. Copyright © Lochlainn Seabrook.

ROYAL GRAMMA

AQUARIUM FISH PROFILE 38
COMMON NAME: Royal gramma.
SCIENTIFIC NAME: *Gramma loreto*.
HABITAT TYPE: Marine; tropical coral reefs and rocky caves.
ORIGIN: Tropical western Atlantic, mainly the Caribbean Sea.
SIZE: Up to 3 in TL.
LIFESPAN: Typically 5–6 years in captivity, longer in optimal reef systems.
COLORATION: Brilliant purple anterior fading to golden yellow posteriorly; eyes and fins bordered with violet highlights.
DIET: Carnivorous; consumes planktonic crustaceans, copepods, brine shrimp, mysis, and finely chopped seafood.
TEMPERAMENT: Generally peaceful but territorial toward similar species.
TANK LEVEL: Mid to lower levels near caves or rock crevices.
MINIMUM TANK SIZE: 30 gallons for one adult.
AQUARIUM CONDITIONS: Temperature 72–80°F; salinity 1.020–1.025; pH 8.1–8.4; well-oxygenated water with live rock and subdued current.
BEHAVIOR: Secretive yet confident once established; often hovers inverted under ledges. Swims slowly and defends a small territory.
BREEDING: Cave spawner; male guards adhesive eggs deposited on substrate or rock surfaces. Hatching occurs within a few days at tropical temperatures.
COMPATIBLE SPECIES: Works well with gobies, clownfish, cardinalfish, firefish, and small wrasses. Avoid housing with aggressive fish such as damselfish or dottybacks.
DIFFICULTY LEVEL: Easy to moderate; hardy once acclimated. Accepts prepared foods readily.
POPULARITY: Highly popular among marine aquarists for its vivid color, compact size, and tolerance of reef environments.
NOTABLE FEATURES: Exhibits a distinctive bi-colored body pattern and hovering posture. Serves as a natural cleaner, removing parasites from tank mates. Its small size, bright contrast, and resilience make it ideal for nano reefs. A single specimen can become the visual centerpiece of smaller aquariums. When alarmed, it retreats quickly to its chosen cave or crevice. In the wild, it inhabits coral outcrops at depths of 1–200 ft, forming loose colonies among reef slopes. This species is reef-safe and rarely disturbs invertebrates. In nature, it contributes to the health of coral ecosystems through parasite removal.

Royal gramma, *Gramma loreto*. Copyright © Lochlainn Seabrook.

SAILFIN TANG

AQUARIUM FISH PROFILE 39
COMMON NAME: Sailfin tang.
SCIENTIFIC NAME: *Zebrasoma veliferum*.
HABITAT TYPE: Marine; sheltered lagoons and seaward reefs with abundant coral and algae; often grazes along reef slopes in moderate currents.
ORIGIN: Western Pacific and Indian Oceans, from Indonesia and the Philippines to the Great Barrier Reef.
SIZE: Up to 15 in TL. Adults in aquariums often reach about 12 in.
LIFESPAN: 10–15 years in captivity with proper diet and stable water.
COLORATION: Olive to brown body with vertical yellow stripes and light horizontal bands; dorsal and anal fins display alternating dark and light markings that intensify with age. Juveniles are lighter and more translucent, with color deepening in dominant adults.
DIET: Herbivorous; feeds on filamentous algae, seaweed, and marine greens. Supplement with spirulina and blanched vegetables.
TEMPERAMENT: Peaceful but territorial toward other tangs of similar shape or color. May chase smaller algae grazers in tight spaces.
TANK LEVEL: Mid to upper levels. Spends most of the day cruising through open areas.
MINIMUM TANK SIZE: 180 gallons. Larger aquariums improve stability and reduce aggression.
AQUARIUM CONDITIONS: Temperature 74–82°F, pH 8.1–8.4, specific gravity 1.020–1.025, strong current, and ample live rock for grazing. Maintain excellent oxygenation.
BEHAVIOR: Constant grazer and active swimmer; extends fins when threatened to appear larger; prefers open water with hiding spaces. May form small loose groups in the wild.
BREEDING: Rarely achieved in aquariums; external spawner releasing eggs into open water at dusk.
COMPATIBLE SPECIES: Peaceful reef-safe fish such as clownfish, chromis, and cardinalfish; avoid triggers and large angelfish.
DIFFICULTY LEVEL: Moderate to advanced; requires excellent water quality and an algae-based diet.
POPULARITY: Highly sought by marine aquarists for its striking pattern and graceful swimming.
NOTABLE FEATURES: Possesses a sharp caudal spine for defense and a large sail-like dorsal fin that expands when displaying; one of the most impressive tangs in the aquarium trade.

Sailfin tang, *Zebrasoma veliferum*. Copyright © Lochlainn Seabrook.

SCARLET BADIS

AQUARIUM FISH PROFILE 40
COMMON NAME: Scarlet badis.
SCIENTIFIC NAME: *Dario dario*.
HABITAT TYPE: Freshwater; plant-filled ponds and slow streams.
ORIGIN: Northern India, particularly West Bengal and Assam.
SIZE: Up to 0.8 in TL.
LIFESPAN: About 3 to 5 years.
COLORATION: Males exhibit brilliant red and orange vertical bands with iridescent blue edging on the fins. Females are smaller, with subdued brownish tones and faint striping. Color intensity increases during courtship and dominance displays.
DIET: Micro-predator feeding on small crustaceans, insect larvae, and worms. In aquariums, accepts live or frozen foods such as daphnia and bloodworms.
TEMPERAMENT: Peaceful but territorial toward males of the same species. Best kept singly or in small groups with multiple hiding areas.
TANK LEVEL: Mid to bottom.
MINIMUM TANK SIZE: 10 gallons.
AQUARIUM CONDITIONS: Prefers soft, slightly acidic water between 72–79°F, pH 6.5–7.5, with gentle flow and dense plant cover. Requires fine substrate and shaded lighting to mimic its natural habitat.
BEHAVIOR: Males establish small territories and display flared fins when rival males approach. Spends much time exploring vegetation and crevices. Sensitive to poor water quality and sudden changes.
BREEDING: Bubble-nest spawner. Male guards the nest and fry until free-swimming. Provide dense moss or spawning mops to protect eggs.
COMPATIBLE SPECIES: Suitable with small, calm fish such as neon tetras or pygmy corydoras. Avoid fin-nippers like tiger barbs or active species like danios.
DIFFICULTY LEVEL: Moderate. Requires clean, stable water and regular feeding with live or frozen foods.
POPULARITY: Increasing due to its vivid coloration and small size, ideal for nano aquariums.
NOTABLE FEATURES: Among the smallest known percoid fish. Highly dimorphic with pronounced male coloration and courtship behavior. Displays remarkable intensity of color relative to body size. Thrives in heavily planted, low-flow aquariums that replicate shaded forest streams.

Scarlet badis, *Dario dario*. Copyright © Lochlainn Seabrook.

SIAMESE ALGAE EATER

AQUARIUM FISH PROFILE 41
COMMON NAME: Siamese algae eater.
SCIENTIFIC NAME: *Crossocheilus oblongus*.
HABITAT TYPE: Freshwater; rivers and streams with moderate current and sandy or rocky bottoms.
ORIGIN: Southeast Asia, primarily Thailand, Laos, and Cambodia.
SIZE: Up to 6 in TL.
LIFESPAN: 8–10 years in captivity.
COLORATION: Silver body with a distinct black horizontal stripe running from snout to tail; fins are mostly clear or slightly yellowish. The stripe may fade during stress or dominance displays.
DIET: Omnivorous; feeds on algae, biofilm, and small invertebrates. In aquariums it accepts flakes, wafers, and blanched vegetables.
TEMPERAMENT: Generally peaceful but may become territorial with its own kind in small tanks. Best kept singly or in groups of at least five to reduce aggression.
TANK LEVEL: Bottom to mid-level.
MINIMUM TANK SIZE: 30 gallons for a single specimen; larger tanks preferred for groups.
AQUARIUM CONDITIONS: Temperature 75–79°F, pH 6.5–7.5, soft to moderately hard water, with strong filtration and steady water movement. Provide hiding places such as rocks and driftwood.
BEHAVIOR: Active swimmer that grazes continuously on surfaces. Effective algae controller. Requires secure lid as it may jump when startled. Best maintained in clean, well-oxygenated water.
BREEDING: Rarely achieved in captivity. Breeding occurs in nature during the rainy season in flowing waters. Sexes are similar, with females slightly fuller-bodied.
COMPATIBLE SPECIES: Works well with peaceful community fish such as rasboras, tetras, and gouramis. Avoid housing with large species, or aggressive species like tiger barbs or redtail sharks.
DIFFICULTY LEVEL: Moderate.
POPULARITY: High among aquarists for its algae-eating efficiency and streamlined beauty. Commonly found in pet stores worldwide due to its hardiness.
NOTABLE FEATURES: Efficient algae grazer valued for natural tank maintenance and long lifespan. Streamlined body and strong swimming ability make it a distinctive and elegant addition to large planted aquariums.

Siamese algae eater, *Crossocheilus oblongus*. Copyright © Lochlainn Seabrook.

SIAMESE FIGHTING FISH

AQUARIUM FISH PROFILE 42
COMMON NAME: Siamese fighting fish.
SCIENTIFIC NAME: *Betta splendens*.
HABITAT TYPE: Freshwater; shallow rice paddies, warm ponds.
ORIGIN: Rice paddies, canals, and slow-moving streams of Thailand, Cambodia, Laos, and Vietnam.
SIZE: Males up to 3 in TL; females slightly smaller.
LIFESPAN: Average 3 to 5 years in captivity.
COLORATION: Wide range of vivid hues including red, blue, green, turquoise, orange, yellow, and white, with metallic iridescence. Fins may be veiltail, crowntail, halfmoon, or plakat forms depending on selective breeding, with males brighter.
DIET: Carnivorous; consumes insect larvae, small crustaceans, and zooplankton. In aquariums, thrives on high-protein pellets, frozen bloodworms, and brine shrimp.
TEMPERAMENT: Highly territorial males; aggressive toward other males and similar-looking species. Females generally peaceful when kept in groups with space and cover.
TANK LEVEL: Primarily surface-dwelling; occasionally explores midwater.
MINIMUM TANK SIZE: 5 gallons for a single adult.
AQUARIUM CONDITIONS: Temperature 76–82°F; pH 6.5–7.5; soft to moderately hard water with gentle filtration and minimal current. Requires access to surface air due to labyrinth organ.
BEHAVIOR: Builds bubble nests; responds to surroundings with intelligence and curiosity. Known for flaring fins as a display of dominance or defense.
BREEDING: Male constructs bubble nest; after courtship, eggs are released and fertilized, then guarded by male until hatching. Fry are free-swimming in 2–3 days.
COMPATIBLE SPECIES: Peaceful bottom dwellers such as Corydoras catfish, kuhli loaches, and small snails. Avoid fin-nippers such as tiger barbs, serpae tetras, and black skirt tetras.
DIFFICULTY LEVEL: Easy to moderate; tolerant of varied conditions but sensitive to cold or dirty water.
POPULARITY: One of the most recognizable and frequently kept tropical fish worldwide.
NOTABLE FEATURES: Possesses a labyrinth organ for atmospheric breathing, allowing survival in low-oxygen waters. Males exhibit elaborate finnage and striking color variation developed through centuries of selective breeding.

Siamese fighting fish, *Betta splendens*. Copyright © Lochlainn Seabrook.

SIX-LINE WRASSE

AQUARIUM FISH PROFILE 43
COMMON NAME: Six-line wrasse.
SCIENTIFIC NAME: *Pseudocheilinus hexataenia*.
HABITAT TYPE: Marine; tropical coral reefs and lagoon shallows.
ORIGIN: Indo-Pacific region, from the Red Sea and East Africa to the islands of the central Pacific.
SIZE: Up to 3 in TL.
LIFESPAN: 5 to 10 years in captivity.
COLORATION: The body is vivid orange-pink with six horizontal blue or turquoise lines running from snout to tail. The caudal fin is often translucent with a faint blue margin, and the eye is bright red.
DIET: Carnivorous; feeds on small crustaceans, worms, and other microfauna. Accepts frozen mysis, brine shrimp, and finely chopped seafood in aquariums.
TEMPERAMENT: Generally peaceful toward most species but can become territorial, especially in smaller tanks or with similar-shaped wrasses.
TANK LEVEL: Active throughout the mid to lower levels of the aquarium.
MINIMUM TANK SIZE: 30 gallons.
AQUARIUM CONDITIONS: Temperature 72–78°F; pH 8.1–8.4; salinity 1.020–1.025; well-oxygenated water with strong circulation and ample live rock for grazing and hiding.
BEHAVIOR: Constantly patrols the rockwork, darting in and out of crevices in search of prey. Known to control small pests such as bristle worms and pyramid snails. Can become aggressive if confined or housed with conspecifics.
BREEDING: Rarely achieved in captivity. Pelagic spawner with external fertilization; eggs and larvae are planktonic and difficult to raise.
COMPATIBLE SPECIES: Works well with peaceful reef fish such as clownfish, gobies, and chromis; avoid housing with dottybacks or aggressive damsels.
DIFFICULTY LEVEL: Moderate; requires stable water quality and a covered aquarium to prevent jumping.
POPULARITY: Common and highly favored among reef aquarists for its color, activity, and pest-control benefits.
NOTABLE FEATURES: Six distinct horizontal stripes, quick darting movements, and constant foraging behavior make this species one of the most animated and useful additions to reef systems.

Six-line wrasse, *Pseudocheilinus hexataenia*. Copyright © Lochlainn Seabrook.

SPOTTED MANDARIN

AQUARIUM FISH PROFILE 44
COMMON NAME: Spotted mandarin.
SCIENTIFIC NAME: *Synchiropus picturatus*.
HABITAT TYPE: Marine; sandy coral reefs and tropical lagoons.
ORIGIN: Western Pacific, from the Philippines to the Coral Sea.
SIZE: Up to 3 in TL.
LIFESPAN: 5–7 years in optimal aquarium conditions.
COLORATION: Bright greenish-blue body with orange-rimmed circular spots and blue striping on the face and fins. Iridescent scales create a metallic sheen under aquarium lighting.
DIET: Carnivorous. Consumes copepods, amphipods, and other live microcrustaceans. In captivity, may accept frozen mysis shrimp or enriched brine shrimp after acclimation.
TEMPERAMENT: Peaceful and shy. Should not be kept with aggressive or highly competitive feeders such as damselfish or dottybacks.
TANK LEVEL: Bottom to mid-level.
MINIMUM TANK SIZE: 30 gallons for a single specimen with a mature live rock system.
AQUARIUM CONDITIONS: Temperature 75–82°F, pH 8.1–8.4, salinity 1.020–1.025, moderate water flow, stable reef environment with abundant live rock for grazing.
BEHAVIOR: Constantly glides and hovers near rock surfaces in search of prey. Moves with slow, graceful fin motions and rarely swims in open water.
BREEDING: Spawning occurs at dusk. Pairs ascend in the water column to release eggs and sperm simultaneously. Larvae are pelagic and require planktonic food.
COMPATIBLE SPECIES: Peaceful reef fish such as gobies, clownfish, or firefish. Avoid territorial species that may outcompete for food.
DIFFICULTY LEVEL: Moderate to high. Requires established reef tank and consistent availability of live food sources.
POPULARITY: Highly sought after in the marine aquarium trade for its vivid coloration and gentle nature.
NOTABLE FEATURES: Known for its psychedelic patterning and mucous-covered skin, which protects against parasites and enables it to thrive without scales. Its vivid coloration and unique locomotion make it one of the most photogenic reef fish in the hobby. This species is sometimes called the psychedelic mandarin due to its striking, kaleidoscopic appearance.

Spotted mandarin, *Synchiropus picturatus*. Copyright © Lochlainn Seabrook.

SUNBURST ANTHIAS

AQUARIUM FISH PROFILE 45
COMMON NAME: Sunburst anthias.
SCIENTIFIC NAME: *Serranocirrhitus latus*.
HABITAT TYPE: Marine; warm deep reef slopes and drop-offs.
ORIGIN: Western Pacific Ocean, from southern Japan and the Philippines to Palau and Papua New Guinea.
SIZE: Up to 5 in TL.
LIFESPAN: 5–7 years in captivity with proper care.
COLORATION: Brilliant orange to pink body with golden-yellow shading on the head, chest, and fins. Dorsal and anal fins show violet or magenta edging. Females are lighter with less fin coloration, while males deepen in tone when displaying.
DIET: Carnivorous. In the wild it feeds on zooplankton and small crustaceans. In captivity it accepts mysis shrimp, brine shrimp, finely chopped seafood, and micro-pellets.
TEMPERAMENT: Peaceful and shy. Best kept with calm reef species. Avoid aggressive or fast-feeding fish such as triggerfish or damselfish.
TANK LEVEL: Mid to lower levels, near caves and coral ledges where it seeks shelter.
MINIMUM TANK SIZE: 70 gal.
AQUARIUM CONDITIONS: Temperature 74–80°F; pH 8.1–8.4; specific gravity 1.020–1.025. Moderate water flow and high oxygen levels required. Prefers dim lighting and live rock structure for hiding.
BEHAVIOR: Solitary or found in loose harems. Gentle swimmer that spends most of its time near shelter. Males may guard territories when multiple are housed together.
BREEDING: Protogynous hermaphrodite. All individuals start as females; dominant ones become males. Spawns at dusk in the open water column. Breeding success in captivity is rare.
COMPATIBLE SPECIES: Ideal companions include clownfish, gobies, firefish, and chromis. Avoid fin-nippers such as sergeant majors and dottybacks.
DIFFICULTY LEVEL: Intermediate. Requires stable conditions and consistent feeding.
POPULARITY: Highly sought after for its radiant color and gentle disposition among reef aquarists.
NOTABLE FEATURES: The only member of its genus. Its vivid sunset hues and graceful swimming make it one of the most visually striking anthias species in the aquarium trade.

Sunburst anthias, *Serranocirrhitus latus*. Copyright © Lochlainn Seabrook.

TIGER BARB

AQUARIUM FISH PROFILE 46

COMMON NAME: Tiger barb.
SCIENTIFIC NAME: *Puntigrus tetrazona*.
HABITAT TYPE: Freshwater; clear, slow streams and rivers.
ORIGIN: Indonesia, Malaysia, Borneo, and Sumatra.
SIZE: Up to 3 in TL.
LIFESPAN: About 5 to 7 years in captivity.
COLORATION: Distinctive orange-gold body with four vertical black stripes, red-tipped fins, and an iridescent sheen. Color intensity varies with diet, lighting, and mood. Males display deeper red on snout and fins when breeding, especially under light.
DIET: Omnivorous. Eats flakes, pellets, insects, worms, algae, and plant matter. Appreciates a mixed diet for best color.
TEMPERAMENT: Semi-aggressive. Can nip fins of long-finned fish such as angelfish or bettas. Best kept in groups of six or more to reduce aggression.
TANK LEVEL: Mid to upper levels.
MINIMUM TANK SIZE: 20 gallons for a small school.
AQUARIUM CONDITIONS: Prefers soft to moderately hard water, pH 6.0–8.0, temperature 74–79°F. Provide plants, driftwood, and open swimming space. Gentle current is ideal.
BEHAVIOR: Active schooling fish. Displays constant motion and social hierarchy within the group. Peaceful when maintained in sufficient numbers but may harass slower species.
BREEDING: Egg scatterer. Spawning triggered by warm, clean water and fine-leaved plants or spawning mops. Parents should be removed after spawning to prevent egg predation. Fry hatch in 1–2 days.
COMPATIBLE SPECIES: Works well with zebra danios, cherry barbs, and cory catfish. Avoid slow or long-finned species.
DIFFICULTY LEVEL: Easy. Hardy and adaptable to varied conditions.
POPULARITY: Very popular community fish worldwide due to striking pattern and lively nature.
NOTABLE FEATURES: Recognized instantly by its tiger-like stripes and bold group behavior. One of the most active and visually dynamic barbs in the hobby. Displays complex social interaction within schools, often synchronized in motion. Responds strongly to environmental changes, showing rapid color shifts. Selective breeding has produced green, albino, and long-finned forms, all retaining the species' trademark vigor and beauty.

Tiger barb, *Puntigrus tetrazona*. Copyright © Lochlainn Seabrook.

TWINSPOT GOBY

AQUARIUM FISH PROFILE 47
COMMON NAME: Twinspot goby.
SCIENTIFIC NAME: *Signigobius biocellatus*.
HABITAT TYPE: Marine; sandy lagoons and coastal reef flats with scattered rubble.
ORIGIN: Western Pacific Ocean, from Indonesia to Papua New Guinea and northern Australia.
SIZE: Up to 3.9 in TL.
LIFESPAN: 3–5 years.
COLORATION: Cream to pale brown body marked with dark diagonal bands; each dorsal fin displays a prominent black eye-like spot ringed in blue and yellow; fins often translucent with fine iridescent edging that shimmers under light.
DIET: Carnivorous; feeds on small crustaceans, copepods, and detritus sifted from the substrate.
TEMPERAMENT: Peaceful and shy; best kept singly or as a bonded pair.
TANK LEVEL: Bottom.
MINIMUM TANK SIZE: 30 gal.
AQUARIUM CONDITIONS: Temperature 75–82 °F; salinity 1.020–1.025 SG; pH 8.1–8.4; fine sand substrate; moderate lighting and gentle current; stable, well-oxygenated reef system with ample live rock and open sand areas.
BEHAVIOR: Constantly sifts mouthfuls of sand through gills to extract food; retreats quickly into burrows when alarmed; forms monogamous pairs that share a burrow and guard territory; may rearrange substrate while digging.
BREEDING: Rare in captivity; pairs maintain and defend shared burrows; eggs are laid within the burrow and guarded by the male until hatching.
COMPATIBLE SPECIES: Peaceful reef inhabitants such as firefish, clownfish, and cardinalfish; avoid aggressive bottom dwellers like wrasses or dottybacks.
DIFFICULTY LEVEL: Moderate to difficult; requires fine substrate, stable water chemistry, and frequent small feedings.
POPULARITY: Increasing among advanced reef aquarists for its unique behavior and striking appearance.
NOTABLE FEATURES: Distinctive twin "eye spots" on dorsal fins serve as false targets, thus acting as predator deterrents; continuous sand-sifting keeps substrate clean and aerated; one of few gobies known for lifelong pairing behavior.

Twinspot goby, *Signigobius biocellatus*. Copyright © Lochlainn Seabrook.

YELLOW TANG

AQUARIUM FISH PROFILE 48
COMMON NAME: Yellow tang.
SCIENTIFIC NAME: *Zebrasoma flavescens*.
HABITAT TYPE: Marine; tropical coral reefs and coastal lagoons.
ORIGIN: Coral reefs of Hawaii, Johnston Atoll, and surrounding central Pacific regions.
SIZE: Up to 8 in TL.
LIFESPAN: Commonly 30 years in captivity with proper care.
COLORATION: Uniform bright yellow body and fins, white scalpel-like spine at the tail base, small mouth adapted for grazing. Color may fade slightly at night or under stress, then recovers.
DIET: Primarily herbivorous, feeding on marine algae and seaweed; accepts prepared herbivore flakes and blanched vegetables in aquaria.
TEMPERAMENT: Generally peaceful but territorial toward other tangs; best kept singly unless in very large aquarium systems.
TANK LEVEL: Active midwater swimmer.
MINIMUM TANK SIZE: 100 gallons.
AQUARIUM CONDITIONS: Temperature 75–82°F; pH 8.1–8.4; salinity 1.020–1.025. Requires strong water movement, high oxygenation, and excellent filtration.
BEHAVIOR: Constant grazer, spends the day picking at algae-covered surfaces; may chase conspecifics but rarely harms other species. Speed bursts can reach about 5 mph when startled.
BREEDING: Rare in home aquariums; occurs in the wild through group spawning at dusk with external fertilization.
COMPATIBLE SPECIES: Works well with clownfish, gobies, and angelfish; avoid aggressive species such as triggerfish and large damselfish.
DIFFICULTY LEVEL: Moderate; hardy once acclimated but sensitive to poor water quality.
POPULARITY: Extremely popular and long favored in the marine aquarium trade for its vivid color and resilience.
NOTABLE FEATURES: Recognized by its pure yellow body and retractable defensive caudal spine; a symbol of Hawaiian reef life and one of the most iconic saltwater aquarium fish worldwide. Its constant algae-grazing helps control nuisance growth and maintain reef balance. Active behavior and bright coloration make it a focal point in community tanks. Thrives when given ample swimming space and continuous access to live rock for grazing. Regular seaweed feeding supports digestive health and natural coloration.

Yellow tang, *Zebrasoma flavescens*. Copyright © Lochlainn Seabrook.

ZEBRA DANIO

AQUARIUM FISH PROFILE 49

COMMON NAME: Zebra danio.
SCIENTIFIC NAME: *Danio rerio*.
HABITAT TYPE: Freshwater; clear, slow streams and ponds.
ORIGIN: Streams, rice paddies, and slow-moving waters of India, Bangladesh, Nepal, and Myanmar.
SIZE: Up to 2.5 in TL.
LIFESPAN: Typically 3–5 years, occasionally up to 6 in ideal care.
COLORATION: Silvery-white body with five horizontal blue-violet stripes running from gill cover to tail fin; fins translucent to pale yellow; males slimmer and more vividly striped than females; especially noticeable in sunlight.
DIET: Omnivorous; accepts flakes, small pellets, brine shrimp, daphnia, and bloodworms.
TEMPERAMENT: Peaceful, active schooling fish; best kept in groups of six or more to reduce stress.
TANK LEVEL: Mid to upper levels.
MINIMUM TANK SIZE: 20 gal long for a small school.
AQUARIUM CONDITIONS: Temperature 72–78 °F; pH 6.5–7.5; moderate water flow with good oxygenation; subdued to moderate lighting.
BEHAVIOR: Constant swimmer; prefers open areas for schooling; may jump if startled, so a secure lid is essential.
BREEDING: Egg scatterer; pairs spawn at dawn among fine-leaved plants or mesh; adults should be removed post-spawning to prevent egg predation. Fry hatch within 48 hours and require microscopic foods initially.
COMPATIBLE SPECIES: Suitable with peaceful community fish such as neon tetras, cory catfish, guppies, and harlequin rasboras. Avoid housing with fin-nippers like tiger barbs and red-tail sharks.
DIFFICULTY LEVEL: Easy; tolerant of varying water conditions and ideal for beginners.
POPULARITY: One of the most common and enduring freshwater aquarium species worldwide.
NOTABLE FEATURES: Hardy, fast-swimming species widely used in biological research; notable for its bold horizontal striping and continuous motion that adds vitality to community aquariums. Known for its social intelligence and cooperative schooling behavior. Highly adaptable and responsive to environmental cues, making it a model species for aquarists and scientists alike. Its resilience, beauty, and grace make it a timeless aquarium favorite.

Zebra danio, *Danio rerio*. Copyright © Lochlainn Seabrook.

ZEBRA PLECO

AQUARIUM FISH PROFILE 50
COMMON NAME: Zebra pleco.
SCIENTIFIC NAME: *Hypancistrus zebra*.
HABITAT TYPE: Freshwater; clear, fast-flowing freshwater rivers with rocky substrates.
ORIGIN: Rio Xingu, Pará, Brazil, South America.
SIZE: Up to 3.2 in TL.
LIFESPAN: 10–15 years.
COLORATION: Alternating black-and-white horizontal bands covering the body and fins; eyes dark with metallic reflection.
DIET: Omnivorous; feeds on insect larvae, small crustaceans, and protein-rich prepared foods.
TEMPERAMENT: Peaceful and secretive.
TANK LEVEL: Bottom.
MINIMUM TANK SIZE: 20 gal for a small group.
AQUARIUM CONDITIONS: Soft, warm, oxygen-rich water; temperature 80–86 °F; pH 6.0–7.5; strong filtration, moderate current, and frequent water changes.
BEHAVIOR: Nocturnal; rests in rock crevices by day; emerges at night to feed; highly territorial males guard chosen caves.
BREEDING: Cave spawner; female deposits adhesive eggs in the male's cave; male guards eggs and fry until free-swimming after 7–10 days.
COMPATIBLE SPECIES: Peaceful companions include neon tetras, rasboras, and corydoras. Avoid aggressive or fin-nipping tankmates such as tiger barbs or serpae tetras.
DIFFICULTY LEVEL: Moderate; sensitive to low oxygen and unstable water quality.
POPULARITY: Very high; prized for rarity, elegance, and striking pattern; one of the most coveted plecos worldwide.
NOTABLE FEATURES: Distinct zebra striping and compact body; adapted for strong currents with flattened shape and wide pectoral fins; endemic to the Xingu River basin; now endangered due to hydroelectric dam construction. Thrives in well-oxygenated aquaria with shaded caves; males develop longer odontodes on cheeks during breeding; known for calm demeanor and slow movement; requires pristine conditions for long-term health. Rediscovered in captivity after near disappearance from export trade; ideal showcase species for advanced aquarists; symbolizes conservation challenges facing South American freshwater fauna. A living reminder of the fragility of tropical river ecosystems.

Zebra pleco, *Hypancistrus zebra*. Copyright © Lochlainn Seabrook.

The End

MEET THE AUTHOR

LOCHLAINN SEABROOK is a prolific lifelong researcher, historian, author, artist, and composer whose knowledge and experience span numerous fields. His remarkable productivity stems from his broad interests, decades of meticulous research, and an unwavering daily devotion to writing and creative exploration.

The idea of specializing in a single subject is a modern invention. In the spirit of the great polymaths—Aristotle, Isaac Newton, Benjamin Franklin, and Thomas Jefferson—Seabrook works across dozens of disciplines, with intellectual pursuits encompassing history, science, philosophy, religion, and the arts. The result is an expansive body of original writings that distill years of careful analysis into clear, accessible language for the general reader.

Rejecting the narrow confines of modern specialization, Seabrook views all knowledge as intrinsically interconnected. This integrative vision, combined with long hours of focused, solitary study and a rigorous work ethic, has enabled him to produce an extraordinary corpus of literature uniting the sciences and the humanities—a natural outgrowth of a lifetime devoted to inquiry, creativity, and the preservation of evidence-based history.

AMERICAN POLYMATH LOCHLAINN SEABROOK is a bestselling author, award-winning historian, and acclaimed multidisciplinary artist. A descendant of the families of Alexander Hamilton Stephens, John Singleton Mosby, Edmund Winchester Rucker, and William Giles Harding, the neo-Victorian scholar is a 7th generation Kentuckian, and one of the most prolific and widely read traditional writers in the world today. Known by literary critics as the "new Shelby Foote," the "American Robert Graves," the "Southern Joseph Campbell,"

and the "Rocky Mountain Richard Jefferies," and by his fans as the "the best author ever," he is a recipient of the United Daughters of the Confederacy's prestigious Jefferson Davis Historical Gold Medal, and is considered the foremost Southern interpreter of American Civil War history—or what he refers to as the War for the Constitution (1861-1865).

A lifelong litterateur, the Sons of Confederate Veterans member has authored and edited books ranging in topics from ancient and modern history, politics, science, comparative religion, diet and nutrition, spirituality, astronomy, entertainment, military, biography, mysticism, anthropology, cryptozoology, photography, and Bible studies, to natural history, technology, paleography, music, humor, gastronomy, etymology, paleontology, onomastics, mysteries, alternative health and fitness, wildlife, alternate history, comparative mythology, genealogy, Christian history, and the paranormal; books that his readers describe as "game changers," "transformative," and "life altering."

One of America's most popular living historians, nature writers, and Transcendentalists, he is a 17th generation Southerner of Appalachian heritage who descends from dozens of patriotic Revolutionary War soldiers and Confederate soldiers from Kentucky, Tennessee, North Carolina, and Virginia. Also a history, wildlife, and nature preservationist, the well-respected scrivener began life as a child prodigy, later maturing into an archetypal Renaissance Man.

Besides being cofounder and co-CEO of Sea Raven Press, an accomplished writer, author, historian, biographer, lexicographer, encyclopedist, neologist, publisher, editor, poet, polymathic creative, onomastician, etymologist, and Bible authority, the influential prosateur is also a Kentucky Colonel, eagle scout, entrepreneur, businessman, composer, screenwriter, nature, wildlife, and landscape photographer, videographer, and filmmaker, artist, artisan, painter, watercolorist, sculptor, ceramic artist, visual artist, sketch artist, pen and ink artist, graphic artist, graphic designer, book designer, book formatter, editorial designer, book cover designer, publishing designer, Web designer, poster artist, digital artist, cartoonist, content creator, inventor, aquarist, genealogist, ufologist, jewelry designer, jewelry maker, former history museum docent, teacher's assistant, and a former Red Cross certified lifeguard, ranch hand, zookeeper, and wrangler. A contemporary songwriter (of some 3,000 songs in a dozen genres), he is also a pianist, organist, drummer, bass player, rhythm guitarist, rhythm mandolinist, percussionist, electronic musician, synthesist, clavichordist, harpsichordist, classical composer, jingle composer, film composer (currently his musical work has been featured in 11 movies), lyricist, band leader, multi-instrument musician, lead vocalist, backup vocalist, session player, music producer, and recording studio mixing engineer, who has worked and performed with some of Nashville's top musicians and singers.

Currently Seabrook is the multi-genre author and editor of over 100 adult and children's books (totaling some 30,000 pages and 15,000,000 words) that have earned him accolades from around the globe. His works, which have sold on every continent except Antarctica, have introduced hundreds of thousands to vital facts that have been left out of our mainstream books. He has been endorsed internationally by leading experts, museum curators, award-winning historians, chart-topping authors, celebrities, filmmakers, noted scientists, well regarded educators, TV show hosts and producers, renowned military artists, venerable heritage organizations, and distinguished academicians of all races, creeds, and colors.

He currently holds two interesting world records: He is the author of the most books on American military officer Nathan Bedford Forrest, and he was the first to publicize and describe the 19th-Century platform reversal of America's two main political parties, namely that Civil War era Democrats (primarily in the South—the Confederacy) were Conservatives, while Civil War era Republicans (primarily in the North—the Union) were Liberals.

Of northern, western, and central European ancestry, he is the 6th great-grandson of the Earl of Oxford and a descendant of European royalty through his Kentucky father and West Virginia mother. A proud descendant of Appalachian coal miners, trainmen, mountain folk, and wilderness pioneers, his modern day cousins include: Johnny Cash, Elvis Presley, Lisa Marie Presley, Billy Ray and Miley Cyrus, Patty Loveless, Tim McGraw, Lee Ann Womack, Dolly Parton, Pat Boone, Naomi, Wynonna, and Ashley Judd, Ricky Skaggs, the Sunshine Sisters, Martha Carson, Chet Atkins, Patrick J. Buchanan, Cindy Crawford, Bertram Thomas Combs (Kentucky's 50th governor), Edith Bolling (second wife of President Woodrow Wilson), Andy Griffith, Riley Keough, George C. Scott, Robert Duvall, Reese Witherspoon, Lee Marvin, Rebecca Gayheart, and Tom Cruise.

A constitutionalist, avid outdoorsman, wilderness conservationist, and gun rights advocate, Seabrook is the author of the international blockbuster, *Everything You Were Taught About the Civil War is Wrong, Ask a Southerner!* He lives with his wife and family in the magnificent Rocky Mountains, heart of the American West, where you will find him writing, hiking, and filming.

For more information on Mr. Seabrook visit
LochlainnSeabrook.com

Praise for Author-Historian-Artist
Lochlainn Seabrook

"Bestselling author, award-winning historian, and esteemed nature writer Lochlainn Seabrook straddles multiple genres with ease, seamlessly weaving together history, science, politics, philosophy, and spirituality with the authority of a scholar and the flair of a storyteller." — SEA RAVEN PRESS

COMMENTS FROM OUR READERS AROUND THE WORLD

★ "Lochlainn Seabrook is a genius writer!" — STEVEN WARD

★ "Best author ever." — EMILY

★ "We get asked a lot what books we use and read. We don't do many modern historians, but we make an exception for some, and Lochlainn Seabrook is one of them. His works are completely well researched from original documents, and heavily footnoted and documented." — SOUTHERN HISTORICAL SOCIETY

★ "Looking forward to more Lochlainn Seabrook books, my favourite historian!" — ALBERTO IGLESIAS

★ "Lochlainn Seabrook is one of the finest authors on true history in this century. His books should be on every student's desk." — RONDA SAMMONS RENO

★ "All of Col. Seabrook's books are great. I have bought most of them and want to end up buying them all." — DAVID VAUGHN

★ "Lochlainn pulls together such arcane facts with relative ease, compiling these into ordinary prose that strike to the heart with substance, no fluff-speak. I am awestruck! Really. He is an inspiration to me. . . . He is truly a revolutionist. He dares to speak what others whisper; he writes with a boldness and an authoritative knowledge that is second to none." — JAY KRUIZENGA

★ "Mr. Lochlainn Seabrook is . . . the most well researched and heavily documented author I've ever read. His books are must haves. Everything he writes should be required reading! I assure you, you won't be disappointed. One simply cannot go wrong with his books. Mr. Seabrook is awesome! . . . I have never read any other author as well researched and footnoted as him. I've been in love with Mr. Seabrook for almost 5 years now. His quick wit and logic is enough reason to purchase his books. But the mere fact that he's so extensively researched is icing on the cake. Mr. Seabrook is my favorite, hands down." — LANI BURNETTE RINKEL

★ "My favorite book is the Bible. Lochlainn Seabrook wrote my second favorite book." — RICHARD FINGER

★ "I have a new favorite author and his name is Lochlainn Seabrook." — J. EWING

★ "Lochlainn Seabrook is an incredible writer and I love all of his books on the South. . . . His writing is brilliant. . . . I look forward to reading more of his masterpieces. Thank you." — JOEY

★ "It's hard to choose just one of Lochlainn's books!" — ROSANNE STEELE

★ "Mr. Seabrook, thank you ever so much for blessing us with your most enlightening works." — LAURENCE DRURY

★ "I recommend anything written by Lochlainn Seabrook." — HOTRODMOB

★ "Awesome books . . . by a great writer of truth, Lochlainn. Thank you so much. Keep up the great work you do." — WILDBUNCH19INF

★ "I love Lochlainn Seabrook's style and approach. It's not the 'norm.' What a miracle his books are. . . . He is a literal life changing author! Amazing books!" — KEITH PARISH

✯ "I adore Mr. Seabrook's style and I love his books. I love an author that does proper research, and still finds a way to engage the reader. Mr. Seabrook does an admirable job of both." — DONALD CAUL

✯ "Lochlainn Seabrook's books are much more well researched and authoritative than those eminently celebrated as being the authorities on the subjects he writes on. You can always trust to find the truth in his writings. . . . He does not rewrite history, but instead shows it as it is." — GARY STIER

✯ "I love all of Colonel Seabrook's books. They are informative and enlightening, and his warm Southern hospitality writing style makes you feel right at home." — KEITH CRAVEN

✯ "Lochlainn Seabrook's work is an absolute treasure of scholarship and historic scope." — MARK WAYNE CUNNINGHAM

✯ "Mr. Seabrook's command of . . . history is breathtaking. . . . He deserves great renown—check out his books!" — MARGARET SIMMONS

✯ "I love Seabrook's writings. LOVE!!! . . . So grateful to know the truth! Keep writing Lochlainn!!!" — REBECCA DALRYMPLE

✯ "Lochlainn Seabrook . . . [has] probably [written] the best book on mental science in existence by a living author. Along with Thomas Troward, Emmet Fox, and Jack Addington, Mr. Seabrook is one of the top four mental science authors of all time, since biblical times." - IAN BARTON STEWART

✯ "Glad I discovered Mr. Seabrook! . . . He writes eye opening books! Unbelievable the facts he unearths - and he backs it all up with truth, notes, footnotes, and bibliography! . . . He always amazes me! His books always see the whole picture. His timelines and bibliographies are incredible. He always provides carefully reasoned arguments! He's the best. To me I think he's better than the late great Shelby Foote! America needs more like Lochlainn Seabrook. I can't wait to own all of his books on the war someday. Everyone who wants the Truth, who seeks the Truth and wants the full story, should read his books." — JOHN BULL BADER

✯ "I love all of Colonel Seabrook's books!" — DEBBIE SIDLE

✯ "Amazing books for unreconstructed people who actually want to know the TRUTH. Seabrook's skill in writing and researching has no equal since the great Shelby Foote. If I could rate his books more than five stars I would." — CANDICE

✯ "Lochlainn Seabrook is well educated and versed in what he writes and I'm impressed with the delivery." — THOMAS L. WHITE

✯ "Lochlainn Seabrook is the author of great works of scholarship." — JOHN B.

✯ "Thank you Lochlainn Seabrook for your wonderful books! You are the real deal! You are an amazing author and I love your books!!" — SOPHIA MEOW CELLIST

✯ "I really enjoy Mr. Seabrook's books! His knowledge is beyond belief!" — SANDRA FISH

✯ "Love Lochlainn Seabrook. Awesome!!" — ROBIN HENDERSON ARISTIDES

✯ "Kudos to Lochlainn Seabrook who is a very good and informative professional truthful historian. We need more like him!" — AMY VACHON

Nurture Your Mind, Body, and Spirit!

READ THE BOOKS OF

SEA RAVEN PRESS

Visit our Webstore for a wide selection of wholesome, family-friendly, evidence-based, educational books for all ages. You'll be glad you did!

Artisan-Crafted Books & Merch From the Rocky Mountains

THANK YOU FOR SUPPORTING OUR SMALL AMERICAN FAMILY BUSINESS!

SeaRavenPress.com

Visit our sister sites:
LochlainnSeabrook.com
YouTube.com/user/SeaRavenPress
YouTube.com/@SeabrookFilms
Rumble.com/user/SeaRavenPress
Pond5.com/artist/LochlainnSeabrook

Red spotted discus, *Symphysodon aequifasciatus* — selectively bred color variant of the blue discus. Copyright © Lochlainn Seabrook.

If you enjoyed this book you will be interested in some of Colonel Seabrook's popular related titles:

- The 50 Greatest Sharks of All Time: A Visual Guide to the Ocean's Apex Predators
- When Monsters Ruled: The 25 Scariest Animals of the Prehistoric World
- The Concise Book of Owls: A Guide to Nature's Most Mysterious Birds
- Rocky Mountain Equines: A Photographic Collection of Horses, Donkeys, and Mules of the American West
- Rocky Mountain Bison: A Photographic Collection of Bison of the American West
- The Cryptid Files Unsealed: An Illustrated Guide to the World's Most Terrifying Unknown Creatures
- The Concise Book of Tigers: A Guide to Nature's Most Remarkable Cats
- North America's Amazing Mammals: An Encyclopedia for the Whole Family

Available from Sea Raven Press and wherever fine books are sold

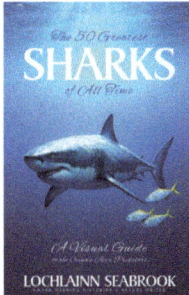

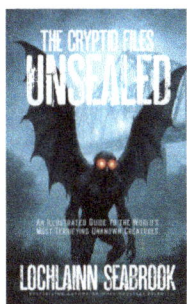

PLEASE VISIT OUR WEBSTORE FOR A COMPLETE LIST OF COLONEL SEABROOK'S BOOKS, AS WELL AS HIS FINE ART NATURE & WILDLIFE PHOTO PRINTS, WALL POSTERS, AND BUMPER STICKERS

SeaRavenPress.com

www.ingramcontent.com/pod-product-compliance
Lightning Source LLC
Chambersburg PA
CBHW042141160426
43201CB00021B/2361